To Josh,
Happy 10th Birthday!

Love,
Jack Bristowe

November 2016

HAMPSHIRE CRICKET
Miscellany

HAMPSHIRE CRICKET
Miscellany

Hampshire Trivia, History, Facts & Stats

ALAN EDWARDS

HAMPSHIRE CRICKET
Miscellany
Hampshire Trivia,
History, Facts & Stats

All statistics, facts and figures are correct as of 1st January 2014

© Alan Edwards

Alan Edwards has asserted his rights in accordance with the Copyright,
Designs and Patents Act 1988 to be identified as the author of this work.

Published By:
Pitch Publishing (Brighton) Ltd
A2 Yeoman Gate
Yeoman Way
Durrington
BN13 3QZ

Email: info@pitchpublishing.co.uk
Web: www.pitchpublishing.co.uk

Published 2014

A catalogue record for this book is available from the British Library.

ISBN 9781909178595

Typesetting and origination by Pitch Publishing.
Printed in Great Britain by CPI Group.

DEDICATION

To all the Hampshire cricketers who have given me so much joy.

ACKNOWLEDGMENTS

Thanks are extended to Paul and Jane Camillin and Gareth Davis of Pitch Publishing, as well as Dean Rockett and Alan Wares for all their help and guidance in the publication of this book. The author also profoundly thanks Dave Allen, the hon curator at Hampshire Cricket, and Innes Marlowe for supplying the photographs. Finally, the book would not have seen the light of day without the support, patience and IT expertise of Andy Ray and the keyboard skills of the author's wife, Jennie.

ABBREVIATIONS

List A matches: Officially recorded limited-overs matches
ODIs: One-day internationals
T20: Twenty20 matches

BIBLIOGRAPHY

In drafting this work, the author referred to many books in his reference library, but special mention must be made of:

Hampshire Handbooks (1950–2012)
Hampshire County Cricket Club: 100 Greats by Neil Jenkinson, Dave Allen and Bill Ricquier (Tempus Books 2003)
The History of Hampshire CCC by Peter Wynne-Thomas (Christopher Helm 1988)
Hampshire County Cricket Club by H.S. Altham, John Arlott, Desmond Eagar and Roy Webber (Phoenix Sports Books 1958)
Who's Who of Cricketers by Philip Bailey, Philip Thorn and Peter Wynne-Thomas (Hamlyn 1993)
Wisden Cricketers' Almanack (various editions)
Important Matches and First-Class Match Scores 1772–1925 (Association of Cricket Statisticians and Historians)
First-Class Cricket: A Complete Record 1926–1939 – compiled and edited by Jim Ledbetter (ACS, Limlow Books and Breedon Books Sport)
The Wisden Book of Cricketers' Lives
Among the periodicals consulted were *The Cricketer, Playfair Cricket Monthly, Wisden Cricket Monthly, Wisden Cricketer, The Cricket Statistician, The Journal of The ACS*. The author's own articles in the newsletters of the Hampshire Cricket Society (1982–20123) were also drawn upon extensively. The Cricket Archive and Cricinfo websites were also of immense value.

INTRODUCTION

This book is the companion to *Hampshire Cricket On This Day*, published in 2012. It is divided into five sections: the first-class game, limited-overs cricket, Twenty20, women's cricket and disability cricket. In the Hampshire context, the last four categories have never been covered in their entirety in a publication before.

With regard to first-class cricket, while those great players of the past are rightly celebrated, so are those who have entertained us in the modern era since 1993, the year that the four-day championship was introduced. Current players can never hope to match the aggregates and appearances of those in the past as they play so many fewer matches. The span of activity is also much shorter. Many tables and entries which cover the whole period of Hampshire's history therefore give the same details for players appearing since 1993. Those figures are not intended as a comparator, but to give a benchmark to which the successors of today's players may aspire.

Hampshire have achieved so much in the last 51 years since Colin Ingleby-Mackenzie's side won the first championship in 1961. There have been three eras since. Richard Gilliat's side won a further championship in 1973 and were cruelly robbed by rain of another in the following year. Cricket has seldom known such grand larceny. They then finished third in 1975. His teams then secured two Sunday League titles. Mark Nicholas took Hampshire to the promised land of three Lord's finals, and the county won them all. The Ageas Bowl era almost suspends belief. In nine years since 2005, Hampshire have played four Lord's finals and four Twenty20 finals days; five triumphs have resulted. Intoxicating days indeed.

All of these wonderful occasions are covered in the book. It also celebrates the four historic grounds at Bournemouth, Southampton, Portsmouth and Basingstoke, as well as, of course, the Ageas Bowl. The current ground has an astonishing history already, particularly in the staging of a Test match, a number of one-day internationals (men and women) and two Twenty20 finals days. And let's not forget those occasions under the floodlights which create such a unique atmosphere. The biographies also feature a number of players of the last 20 years.

It has been a joy to recall the great performances and occasions in Hampshire's history. The entries in the latter part demonstrate just how much cricket, and Hampshire, have progressed.

JIMMY ADAMS

For the past five seasons, Jimmy Adams has been one of the heaviest scorers in county cricket. He achieved the now relatively rare feat of scoring 1,000 runs in the 2009, 2010 and 2012 seasons. In 2011 he was only 65 short. The fair-haired left-handed opening batsman also reached the milestone in 2006. He is the only Hampshire batsman to score 1,000 runs in a season on four occasions since the introduction of the four-day County Championship in 1993. He has been responsible for four of the longest innings in the county's history. In 2006, he batted for 445 minutes when scoring 168 not out to take his side to an unlikely five-wicket victory while chasing down 404 against Yorkshire at Headingley. Soon afterwards, he scored a monumental 262 not out in 592 minutes against Nottinghamshire at Trent Bridge. Four years later, he batted for 428 minutes in making 196 at Scarborough. In company with the precocious James Vince, who eased his way to a maiden century (180), Adams added 278, a Hampshire record fourth-wicket partnership. In the following match against Lancashire at Aigburth, Liverpool, he occupied the crease for a county record 635 minutes in a vain attempt to stave off defeat. He was last out for 194 in the second innings. He also has a share, with Michael Carberry, in Hampshire's record second-wicket partnership of 373 against Somerset at Taunton in 2011. James Henry Kenneth Adams was born in Winchester on 23 September 1980. After captaining England Under-15s, and attending Loughborough University, his career in first-class cricket was a slow burner. He made his Hampshire debut in 2002, but despite those two long innings against Yorkshire and Nottinghamshire in 2006, his place was never secure until 2009. Since then, his heavy scoring has attracted the England selectors. An innings of 142 for England Lions against the Combined Campuses and Colleges in Barbados in February 2011 established his international credentials, but he has since slipped down the pecking order. In his early years he was regarded as a slow scorer, but he has now adapted his game to suit all forms of cricket. He hit two centuries in the Twenty20 competition in 2010, 101 not out against Surrey and an undefeated 100 against Glamorgan, both at the Rose Bowl. He first captained Hampshire when they played in the Caribbean Twenty20 tournament in January 2011, leading them to the final. He obtained the post permanently towards the end of the ensuing summer to become the first Hampshire-born captain since 1939.

By that time, Hampshire's relegation from Division One was virtually a foregone conclusion. While Hampshire struggled to make any headway in Division Two in 2012, he led them to an astonishing victory over county champions Warwickshire in the CB40 final at Lord's at the end of the season. His own part in the match was integral to the success as he top-scored with 66 and captained nervelessly in the field. The achievements of

modern players are often overlooked when compared to some of the past legends but Jimmy Adams has secured an indelible place in the county's history.

AGEAS BOWL

Hampshire's newest ground was opened in 2000, when five second XI matches were played on the nursery ground. It has a considerable and illustrious history already. It has staged Hampshire's inaugural Test match (England v Sri Lanka in 2011), and, as mentioned elsewhere in this book, 17 ODIs and three Twenty20 internationals. It has also hosted two Twenty20 final days, the second of which was won by Hampshire in 2010. The ground, formerly called the Rose Bowl, was obtained on a 999-year lease from Queen's College, Oxford, in 1994. Eastleigh Borough Council granted outline planning permission for the main and nursery grounds in 1996. It was intended to fund the development from the sale of the County Ground in Northlands Road, Southampton. However, a crash in the property market at the time left a £7m funding gap. In August 1996 the National Lottery Sports Fund made an award of £7,176,728. Unfortunately, financial issues have been a constant feature since. It is now hoped that the situation has been stabilised following a ground naming rights partnership deal with Ageas, the insurance company, and a sale/lease-back arrangement with Eastleigh Borough Council which will permit the building of a hotel at the northern end of the ground. The Ageas Bowl's iconic pavilion was formally opened in 2002, flanked by two stands, named after Colin Ingleby-Mackenzie and Shane Warne. On the field, the pitch has not been without its problems. As to be expected on any newly laid square, it took some time to settle down. In the first few years, batsmen were having to cope with variable bounce. The pitch then rolled out to be a belter on which it proved difficult to produce a result in four days.

It is ironic that Hampshire incurred an eight-point deduction in 2011 when they produced a wicket which aided spin from the first morning against Nottinghamshire. Most members felt it was one of the best matches seen on the ground. Though a draw, it was an absorbing contest throughout. The visitors finished four runs short with four wickets in hand. Batsmen have accomplished feats of high achievement at the Ageas Bowl. The encounter with Nottinghamshire in 2005 produced a match of records. Hampshire posted 714/5 declared, their highest ever total. John Crawley made 311 not out, the best score on the ground. The crowd were waiting to applaud his exceeding Dick Moore's record 316, but Shane Warne declared. Hampshire went on to bowl out the champions-elect twice to win by an innings and 188 runs with over a day to spare. They finished 2.5 points adrift of

Nottinghamshire at the top of the table. In 2011, Michael Carberry (300 not out) and Neil McKenzie (237) added a County championship record of 523 for the third wicket against Yorkshire. Left-handed Carberry has made quite a mark. He has a share in Hampshire's best stands for the first four wickets. David Balcombe set a new Ageas Bowl record for Hampshire's bowlers when he recorded 8-71 against Gloucestershire at the start of summer. His match figures of 11-119 are a ground record. One rarity was when the scores finished level. It happened in the second match at the ground against Gloucestershire, in 2001. After rain had curtailed play severely on the first two days, Hampshire were eventually left with ten overs to score 56 to win. Eight runs were required off the last over and three off the last ball, but Dimitri Mascarenhas and Shaun Udal could scamper only two. Hampshire finished on 55/6. The Ageas Bowl has also provided a number of uniquely atmospheric nights under the floodlights, particularly in ODIs and Twenty20 finals. Apart from cricket, the ground has staged some high profile rock concerts, featuring among others, Oasis, REM and Neil Diamond. The REM concert in 2008 meant Hampshire had to move their championship fixture with Durham to Basingstoke.

ALDERSHOT

Hampshire played five matches at The Officers Club Services Ground, Aldershot, in 1905, 1906, 1910 and 1948 (twice). The only century scored by a Hampshire player there was A.J.L. Hill's 113 in the first match, against Surrey.

Charles Llewellyn recorded the best bowling figures when he took 7-45 (13-106 in the match) against Somerset in 1910. The first of the matches in 1948 marked the debut of Derek Shackleton (v Cambridge University). He took 3-47 and 1-46. Five touring sides played against the Army at the ground in the 1930s: India (1932), West Indies (1933 and 1939) and Australia (1934 and 1938). All except the first fixture against the West Indies were one-day friendlies. The match against Australia in 1934 was noteworthy for the appearance of Don Bradman. He hit 79 as the Aussies batted on to entertain the crowd after completing a six-wicket victory. The Pakistanis also played the Combined Services in a one-day friendly in 1974.

ALTON

Hampshire played one first-class match at Alton Recreation Ground, in 1904 against the South Africans. The tourists batted first and totalled 390 (L.J. Tancred 99). Charles Llewellyn took 5-160 against his fellow countrymen. Hampshire were then dismissed for 168 (Bowell 65) and 193 (Sprot 75, Llewellyn 60), to lose by an innings and 19 runs in two days.

AMATEUR SQUASH CHAMPION

Irish-born Tommy Jameson was a tall, powerful right-handed batsman and a good leg-spin bowler who played in 53 matches for Hampshire between 1919 and 1932. He also excelled at racket sports. He won the Amateur Squash Championship in 1922 and 1923 and the Army Singles Racket Championship on three occasions.

MOST APPEARANCES FOR HAMPSHIRE

700 .... Phil Mead
596 .... Alec Kennedy
593 .... Peter Sainsbury
583 .... Derek Shackleton
539 .... George Brown
506 .... Jack Newman
504 .... Roy Marshall

The most appearances by current players are by Dimi Mascarenhas (195), Jimmy Adams (142) and Sean Ervine (129).

APPEARANCES IN MOST TITLE-WINNING SIDES

Three men, David Turner, Paul Terry and Sean Ervine, have played for Hampshire in five title-winning sides.

Turner: County Championship 1973; Sunday League 1975, 1978 and 1986; Benson & Hedges Cup Final 1988

Terry: Sunday League 1978* and 1986; Benson & Hedges Cup Final 1988 and 1992; NatWest Trophy Final 1991

Ervine: C&G Final 2005; FPT Final 2009; Friends Provident Twenty20 Final 2010; Friends Life Twenty20 Final 2012; CB40 Final 2012.

* While Turner was a regular in all the Sunday League–winning sides, Terry played in only two matches in 1978, and was not in the team in the run–in.

WHO WAS HE?

Of all the men to have played first-class cricket for Hampshire, there remains one whose identity has never been established. In Hampshire's match against Somerset at Taunton in 1904, J. Martin batted at number 11, scored 39 and 27, and shared in last-wicket stands of 76 and 48. He also took 1-66 and 4-100. He was, therefore, an able cricketer. However, despite assiduous research by cricket's historians, his biographical details remain a mystery at the time of writing.

THERE'S ONLY ONE BILLY TAYLOR

Only one player has roused Hampshire crowds to song. Whenever he took the ball to bowl, a number of spectators would start to sing 'there's only one Billy Taylor' to the tune of the well-known football anthem. Though Hampshire-born, Taylor played for Sussex between 1999 and 2003, helping them to their first County Championship in the latter year. He had continued to play club cricket for Winchester and Hursley Park in Hampshire and was therefore a popular figure on the county's cricket scene. He played for Hampshire from 2004–2009. In the first of those years, he claimed the first-ever hat-trick at the Rose Bowl while on his way to career best bowling figures of 6-32 against Middlesex. His whole-hearted right arm fast-medium bowling was highly valued by the Hampshire faithful. During the close season he worked as a tree surgeon before becoming a falconer. He is currently on the reserve first-class umpires' list.

ONE APPEARANCE FOR THE COUNTY

Eighty-two players have made only one appearance in first-class cricket for the county since 1895.

ARISTOCRATS

Five Hampshire cricketers played for the county after succeeding to, or being awarded a title: Lionel Tennyson, Sir F.H. Hervey-Bathurst, Sir W.G.H. Jolliffe, Sir J.B. Mill and Sir M. Wood. The last four named all played in the 19th century.

JOHN ARLOTT – SUBSTITUTE FIELDER

John Arlott, that great radio commentator, fielded as a substitute for Hampshire at Worcester in 1938. He wore 'Lofty' Herman's boots – which were one and a half sizes too large for him, and borrowed flannels. Arlott was a Southampton policeman at the time and went down to Worcester to watch the match.

AUSTRALIAN ABORIGINES

The first touring team to visit Hampshire were the Australian Aborigines in 1868. They played three matches. Two were against East Hampshire at Southsea, and they lost the first but won the second handsomely. They owed their victory to Twopenny, who took nine wickets for nine runs in the first innings (and caught the other man) and then returned 5-7 in the second. The third match, against the Gentlemen of Hampshire at the Antelope Ground, was drawn. Twopenny was again in devastating form with the ball as he clean-bowled nine batsmen at a personal cost of 17 runs in the first innings and then took 3-39 in the second.

THE AUSTRALIANS

Between 1896 and 2001, Hampshire played the Australians 26 times. Two matches were won, 13 lost and 11 drawn. One match was abandoned. The county's two victories were in 1912 at Southampton (by eight wickets) and in 2001 at the Rose Bowl (by two wickets). Hampshire also played host to the Australian Imperial Forces in 1919, in a game that was drawn, and Young Australia in 1995 in which the tourists claimed victory by ten wickets.

HAMPSHIRE PLAYER KEEPS WICKET FOR THE AUSTRALIANS

Hector Henry Hyslop was Hampshire-born, in Southampton, in 1840 and played seven matches for the county in 1876–77. He also kept wicket in an emergency for the 1878 and 1886 Australians in England, it being thought that he was born in Australia! He died by his own hand in Cosham in 1920.

KEITH MILLER IN SOUTHAMPTON'S PARKS

The great Australian all-rounder first entered the public consciousness in this country when he was selected for the RAF – comprising both Englishmen and Australians – against a Parks XI in May 1943. He had only arrived in the UK two months before and despite having played first-class cricket in Australia before the Second World War, he was virtually unknown in England. Miller arrived at the ground in khaki shorts with a pair of boots slung over his shoulders. He played in his shorts, Air Force-issue socks and a borrowed sweater (he was shirtless) and, on a mud heap, bowled very quickly. Although he dismissed six batsmen his team were defeated by their opponents, who included five Hampshire players, by two wickets.

AUSTRALIAN BLUSHES

Hampshire have twice bowled out the Aussies for less than 100. In 1985, Kevan James took 6-22 as they were dismissed for 76. Facing Hampshire's 221, the follow-on was only averted in unusual circumstances by their wicketkeeper Wayne Phillips. He had gone to hospital for a precautionary x-ray on a hand, got lost in rush-hour traffic, and arrived just in time to bat last and hit two sixes. In their second innings, the Aussies collapsed again to 126-7 (needing 210). Murray Bennett and Craig McDermott batted out the final 13 overs. When Australia were defeated in 2001, they were bowled out on the stroke of lunch on the first day for 97 (Alan Mullally with 5-18).

JOHNSTON DISMISSED!

In 1953, the Australian tail-ender, Bill Johnston, a natural number 11, contrived with the help of his colleagues to end the season with an average of 102. The only time he was dismissed was against Hampshire when he was caught and bowled by Vic Cannings for eight.

THE INVINCIBLES

Hampshire were the only county to head the Australian 'Invincibles' side of 1948 on first innings. The Australians are so called as they never lost a match. On a difficult, drying pitch, Hampshire batted first after losing the toss and made 195 (Bill Johnston 6-74). They then bowled out the visitors for 117 with the spinners Charles Knott (5-57) and Jim Bailey (4-27) doing the damage. The total would have been even lower had not Keith Miller hit Knott for three successive sixes. Miller (5-25) and Johnston then effectively decided the match by bowling out Hampshire for 103. Though they lost Sidney Barnes to the third ball of their second innings, the pitch had dried out and Australia raced to 182/2 in 132 minutes to win by eight wickets.

DON BRADMAN

Donald Bradman did not play in the above match, the only time he did not play at Southampton. On his three previous visits he scored centuries in 1930 and 1938, reaching the coveted 1,000 runs by the end of May on both occasions. In 1934 he was dismissed for a second ball duck, caught at slip by Philip Mead off the bowling of Giles Baring. He was anxious that his side did not lose in 1948, and kept in constant contact with stand-in skipper Lindsay Hassett throughout.

HAMPSHIRE'S FIRST OVERSEAS PLAYER

Hampshire's first overseas player appeared in their inaugural first-class match, against Sussex at The Antelope Ground in 1864. He was John Carr Lord, a Tasmanian right-handed batsman. He was in England to receive his education and staying with his sister, also Tasmanian born, in Southsea. She was married to an English army officer. The 19-year-old Lord opened the first innings and scored 11. He then batted at number ten in the second innings, in which he was four not out. It was his only match for Hampshire. Lord returned to Tasmania shortly afterwards where he became influential in cricketing and racing circles. He played one match for the island against Victoria in 1873 and later appeared in matches against England touring sides led by W.G. Grace and Lord Harris. He died in 1911, aged 66.

AUSTRALIAN OVERSEAS PLAYERS

Including Lord, 13 Australians have played for Hampshire in first-class cricket. In order of appearance they are: Shaun Graf (1980), Matthew Hayden (1997), Shane Warne (2000, 2004-2007), Simon Katich (2003-05 and 2012), Michael Clarke (2004), Shane Watson (2004-05), Andy Bichel (2005), Dominic Thornely (2006), Stuart Clark (2007), Marcus North (2009), Dan Christian (2010), Phil Hughes (2010) and George Bailey (2013). Another three have played for the county in Twenty20 matches only. Two more Australians, Bruce Reid (1988) and Mike Kasprowicz (1998), were due to play for Hampshire as overseas registrations but both withdrew owing to injury.

AUSTRALIAN TEST CRICKETERS

With the exception of Graf, Thornely and Christian, all the above players represented Australia in Test cricket. However, only Warne, Katich and Watson did so as Hampshire players. Warne's appearances while with the county are a complex issue. He joined in 2000 but toured England in 2001. He was due to return in 2003 but was then banned for a drugs offence. He then captained Hampshire between 2004 and 2007. In that period he played in 35 Tests, making his final Test appearance just prior to the latter season. Katich played in eight Tests in his first spell with Hampshire in 2003/04. Watson appeared in one Test in 2004/05. It marked his Test debut.

ONLY PLAYED ONE DAY

Hampshire contracted Marcus North, the left-handed batsman from Western Australia, as their overseas player for the first part of the 2009 season. He duly took the field for the first time in the second match of the season against Warwickshire at Edgbaston. After making 15 on the first day he was then summoned into the Australian limited-overs side in Dubai and flew there that evening. This proved to be the extent of his career with the county. Interestingly, it was agreed that Hampshire could field a replacement, Michael Lumb, who himself was already engaged in a second XI match. He made 84 in the second innings. It was a considerable change of fortune as Lumb had been dismissed for a pair in the first championship match against Worcestershire at the Rose Bowl, and then fell for another duck in the first innings of the second XI game.

TOURED AUSTRALIA

The following Hampshire players went on England Test tours of Australia while they were registered with the county: Phil Mead (1911/12 and 1928/29), Robin Smith (1990/91), David Gower (1990/91), Shaun Udal (1994/95), John Crawley (2002/03), Kevin Pietersen (2006/07), Michael Carberry (2013/14). Tony Middleton toured with England A in 1992/93. E.G. Wynyard was selected for the 1897/98 tour, but had to withdraw because of his army duties.

MOST RUNS IN A MATCH

The burly Australian left-handed opening batsman, Matthew Hayden, scored 235 not out and 119 v Warwickshire at Southampton in 1997 to achieve the highest aggregate in a match by a Hampshire player. He had also run up 118 in a Sunday League match against the same county while the four-day match was in progress.

HARRY BALDWIN

Harry Baldwin is probably best known for the photograph which shows him as a very tubby man hitching up his trousers. A contemporary wrote, 'Just how Harry Baldwin kept his trousers up is nobody's business! He hitched them up as often as Philip Mead used to pull the peak of his cap, that is, every ball bowled. But Harry could bowl slow-medium off-turners all day and with a wicket to suit him was often deadly, being extremely accurate. He was a very delightful character and fond of a glass of beer.' Baldwin played 150 matches for Hampshire and took 580 wickets (average 24.71), with best figures of 8-74 against Sussex at Hove in 1898.

TOURED BANGLADESH

Both Michael Carberry and Kevin Pietersen were in the England tour party to Bangladesh in 2009/10. Carberry had earlier toured the country with England A in 2006/07. The pair are the only Hampshire players to appear in first-class cricket in Bangladesh since it gained its independence from Pakistan in 1976. Mark Nicholas (captain), Tim Tremlett and Chris Smith were due to tour there with England B to play two three-day matches in 1985/86 but Bangladesh withdrew the invitation due to the number of players with South African connections.

MAY'S BOUNTY, BASINGSTOKE

May's Bounty captured the very essence and charm of the County Championship. The intimacy of the ground, brought about by its compactness, its tree-lined perimeter, informal pavilion and constant background hum emanating from the omnipresent entertainment tents, gave it a unique atmosphere and made it an attractive part of the Hampshire cricket calendar. May's Bounty hosted county cricket for almost a century but with several intermissions. Besides the initial match in 1906 only one other match was played before the First World War. That was in 1914 itself. In the inter-war years another five matches were played – one each in 1935, 1936 and 1938 and two in 1937. First-class cricket returned again for one match against Oxford University in 1951 but it was not until 1966 that Hampshire started to play there annually. Prior to the Second World War Hampshire had a disastrous record on the ground. They lost six of their seven matches, three of them by an innings. The county enjoyed better form from 1966 to 2000, losing only five of their 35 matches, a formidable record. The only counties to defeat them during that period were Nottinghamshire (1969), Glamorgan (1975), Gloucestershire (1978), Lancashire (1991) and Yorkshire (1999). Hampshire returned there between 2008 and 2010, when, respectively, they beat Durham, lost to Yorkshire and then drew with the former county. However, with fewer tents, the ground did not have the same magic as in the previous century. There were common threads running through the matches. Very few escaped the rain. Despite the smallness of the ground runs were nearly always hard to come by. Only one double century was scored, 204 not out by Glamorgan's Alan Jones in 1980. All but one of the ten best analyses were returned by fast-medium bowlers. Another Glamorgan player, Malcolm Nash, headed the list. He returned figures of 9-56 in a fine spell of swing bowling in 1975. He took all the wickets to fall to a bowler, the other batsman being run out. The best all-round performance was by Lancashire's Wasim Akram, who scored 122 and then took 5-48 in 1991. Three more of the world's greatest players will have cause to remember the ground for differing reasons. Colin Cowdrey, a great player of fast bowling, was felled by an Andy Roberts bouncer in 1974, and Sachin Tendulkar, when playing for Yorkshire, was bowled for a duck by P.J. Bakker in 1992.

In 1981, with the result no longer in the balance, the Australian fast bowler Jeff Thomson amused the crowd and himself by bowling leg-spinners for Middlesex. Nearly all the great Hampshire players of this century played at May's Bounty. Robin Smith made the ground his own, despite missing several matches while playing for England at Lord's, with which the championship fixture clashed for many years. He scored 977 runs including no fewer than six of Hampshire's 17 centuries. He also recorded the county's highest score (179) at the ground, against Northamptonshire in 1996. That insatiable run-maker, Michael Carberry, scored 162 and 107 in the last match played there. In the first innings he shared a ground record 314 for the second wicket with Michael Lumb (162). Hampshire's best bowling performances were by Kevan James, who enjoyed a purple match against Somerset in 1997 (5-44 and 8-49) and the tragic Arthur Jaques who twice routed Derbyshire in 1914 (8-67 and 6-38). Jaques was killed in the First World War just over a year later. The Sunday at Basingstoke was one of the great social events of the Hampshire season. It was also traditional for many Hampshire players to select the Basingstoke Sunday for their benefit match, such was its crowd appeal. One-day cricket first came to Basingstoke in the form of a Gillette Cup match in 1967 and a Sunday League match was scheduled every year from 1973. Hampshire's record was: played 29, won 16, lost 12, abandoned 1. No résumé of cricket at Basingstoke would be complete without mentioning John Arlott. He watched all his early cricket at May's Bounty and his evocative memories became etched in the consciousness of generations of Hampshire cricket followers.

WOODEN SPOONISTS

The early years of the 20th century were troubled times for Hampshire. The county finished bottom of the County Championship five times in six years – 1900, 1902, 1903, 1904 and 1905. In these seasons, they won a total of only six matches. They failed to register a single victory in 1900, the only occasion in their history when they have done so. Two matches were won in 1902 and 1904, and one in 1903 and 1905. The only other occasion Hampshire were bottom of the County Championship was in 1980, when they won just one match.

BEES STOPPED PLAY

A swarm of bees held up play in the county's opening fixture of the 2002 season at the Rose Bowl, against Leicestershire. Players lay flat on the ground while the bees buzzed around them. Hampshire member and bee-keeper Ray Feltham then came to the rescue. The iconic Rose Bowl pavilion had been opened earlier in the day, but it appears the attraction to the bees was a blue advertising hoarding.

BUTTERFLY STOPPED PLAY

When Charles Knott was bowling to Sir Derrick Bailey in the match against Gloucestershire at Portsmouth in 1951, one delivery struck a butterfly in flight and killed it. The corpse was placed in a matchbox and Charles Knott later had it mounted on the ball.

BORN IN UNUSUAL LOCATIONS

P.J. Bakker	1986–92	Vlaardingen, Holland
Thomas Hansen	1997–99	Glostrup, Denmark
Jon Hardy	1984–85	Nakuru, Kenya
George Heath	1937–49	Hong Kong
Alex Hosie	1913–35	Wenchow, China
Benny Howell	2011	Bordeaux, France
Arthur Jaques	1913–14	Shanghai
Arthur Lewis	1929	Maseru, Basutoland
William Maundrell	1900	Nagasaki, Japan
Nick Pocock	1976–84	Maracaibo, Venezuela
Frank Ryan	1919–20	New Jersey, USA
Lee Savident	1997–2000	Guernsey
Henry Sprinks	1925–29	Alexandria, Egypt
Paul Terry	1978–96	Osnabruck, Germany
Nesbit Wallace	1884	Halifax, Nova Scotia

BORN IN INDIA

Prior to the First World War in particular, Hampshire were very reliant on India-born cricketers who were, in the main, sons of army officers or Indian civil servants. A number then served in the services themselves. A total of 31 players born in India have played for the county.

FIRST THREE IN THE NATIONAL BATTING AVERAGES

In the dismally wet summer of 1912, three Hampshire players, C.B. Fry, A.C. Johnston and Phil Mead, occupied the first three places of the national batting averages. Fry and Mead were also first and second in the averages in 1911, and Mead was top in 1913.

PROGRESSION TO THE CHAMPIONSHIP

1895	10th
1896	8th
1901	7th
1910	6th
1914	5th
1955	3rd
1958	2nd
1961	1st

ABANDONED MATCHES

Eighteen first-class matches involving Hampshire have been abandoned without a ball being bowled. Three of those matches were abandoned in 1903 alone. The last occurrence was in 2001.

FIRST WIN

Hampshire's first win as a first-class county was against Surrey at The Antelope Ground in August 1865. In a low scoring match (Surrey 87 and 101, Hampshire 96 and 93/2), they emerged victorious by eight wickets. It was an astonishing result as Surrey had won the previous encounter a fortnight earlier by an innings and 221 runs.

OLYMPIC GOLD MEDALLIST

Arthur Egerton Knight won a gold medal in the Olympic Games at Stockholm in 1912 as a member of England's victorious football team. He was a left-back who played for Portsmouth between 1909 and 1922. He played as an amateur for all but his last two seasons. He appeared for Hampshire, again as an amateur, in one match in four separate seasons between 1913 and 1923. He captained the side in his last two appearances in 1921 and 1923, while Lionel Tennyson was away.

THIRD IN THE CHAMPIONSHIP

County Championship table 1955:

		P	W	L	D	Tied	Pts
1.	Surrey	28	23	5	0	0	284
2.	Yorkshire	28	21	5	2	0	268
3.	Hampshire	28	16	5	6	1	210
4.	Sussex	28	13	8	6	1	196
5.	Middlesex	28	14	12	2	0	192

Hampshire attained their highest position in the County Championship at the time, comfortably exceeding their previous best of fifth in 1914. They were never in a position to challenge Surrey or Yorkshire for the title but gained the satisfaction of defeating both during their campaign. Their win over Yorkshire at Bradford was their first in Yorkshire since 1932. They beat all the counties, except Warwickshire and Nottinghamshire. They also tied an exciting game against Sussex at Eastbourne. Their 16 victories exceeded the previous record of 14 in 1921. Hampshire played with a dynamism that excited the cricketing public up and down the country. The catalyst for their approach was Roy Marshall, playing his first full season after a two-year residential qualification period. The great Bajan opening batsman put bowling attacks to the sword from the outset and, in doing so, allowed the batsmen who followed to play with more freedom. He headed the batting averages with 1,890 runs at 36.34. For good measure, Marshall also took 25 wickets with his off-breaks at only 11.92. Two other players who made a significant contribution in their first full seasons were Henry Horton, who scored 1,231 runs, and Peter Sainsbury, who claimed 102 wickets. Jimmy Gray settled in as Marshall's opening partner with 1,189 runs. The bowling attack was well balanced and penetrative. Only two centuries were scored against the county all season. All of the seven main bowlers, Derek Shackleton, Vic Cannings, Peter Sainsbury, Malcolm Heath, Gray, Mervyn Burden and Marshall, averaged under 22 runs per wicket. Shackleton took 147 championship wickets, a tally exceeded only by Surrey's Tony Lock. His opening partner, Cannings, collected a further 94 scalps. Another reason for the county's success was consistency of selection. Only 13 players represented Hampshire during the season. The previous record was 17 in 1932. The only downside to the year was that it proved to be Neville Rogers's final season. Hampshire's most reliable batsman over the past decade went out having scored 1,085 runs that summer. A contractual dispute then brought an end to his playing career.

PETER SAINSBURY

After taking 100 wickets in 1955, Peter Sainsbury had to wait until 1971 before performing the feat for the second and final time. He claimed 107 victims in the latter year. Peter Sainsbury made his Hampshire debut against Oxford University at The Parks in 1954, while on National Service. From the moment he left the army shortly afterwards until his retirement in 1976, he was the county's first-choice all-rounder. He was one of those relatively few all-rounders able to hold down a place as a batsman or bowler. Sainsbury was a slow left-arm bowler who teased batsmen with drift and flight, a shrewd middle-order batsman who was always at his best in a crisis, and a quite magnificent fielder, particularly at backward short leg. Perhaps only Paul Terry has been his equal for Hampshire in the fielding sphere. He achieved 1,000 runs in a season on six occasions, as well as seven centuries. His 668 catches are a Hampshire record. Only 20 men have completed their careers with 20,000 runs and 1,000 wickets. Sainsbury is the only member of that group never to have played Test cricket. A panel of experts commissioned by *Wisden Cricket Monthly* named him in their best post-war team of county cricketers never to play for England. He was originally chosen for the 1958/59 tour of Australia but, upon overnight reflection, the selectors changed their minds and Gloucestershire's John Mortimore travelled instead. Sainsbury had to settle for an England A tour of Pakistan in 1955/56, and two appearances as 12th man against New Zealand in 1958. Born in Southampton on 13 June 1934 and of medium height, he is the only Hampshire player to be a member of two championship-winning sides (1961 and 1973). He made immense contributions to both campaigns. He was one of the few of the old school to adapt to one-day cricket, and was an integral member of Hampshire's first one-day trophy side, the John Player League in 1975. Sainsbury still holds the record for the best bowling figures and all-round performance in List A matches. In the winter of 2012 he was named in a best Hampshire XI since the introduction of one-day cricket in 1963. He stayed on the county staff as coach until 1991. In all forms of cricket he scored 21,655 runs and took 1,447 wickets for the county. Only Phil Mead and Alec Kennedy have exceeded his 593 appearances for Hampshire in first-class cricket. He was considerable cricketer who only now is receiving the recognition he deserves.

DEAN PARK, BOURNEMOUTH

Of all Hampshire's former grounds, none evokes more reflective memories than Dean Park, Bournemouth. It was the most attractive of all Hampshire's grounds. Its tree-lined perimeter cocooned it from the outside world. Most memorably, Dean Park was the venue where the county clinched their first and much cherished County Championship in 1961. The second championship was also secured there in 1973, as was Hampshire's second John Player League title in 1978. All of Hampshire's other one-day titles were won on away grounds. There was a considerable sense of loss when the county were no longer able to play there after 1992. The cessation was relatively sudden. Everyone hoped an accommodation could be reached with the owners but it just never happened. Dean Park was laid out for Bournemouth Cricket Club in 1869 and first came into regular use in 1871. The initial first-class match was in 1897, against the touring Philadelphians. Hampshire beat the North Americans by five wickets, with Major John Spens scoring the first century (118 not out) in the county's first innings. Thereafter, Dean Park played host to all the then Test-playing nations, though Australia's appearances were confined to matches against representative sides, rather than Hampshire. The first championship match was against Somerset in 1898. It was part of the first Bournemouth Cricket Week which became a permanent feature in the town's sporting calendar. Somerset (37 matches) and Yorkshire (32) were the most regular visitors. The Yorkshire match was usually in the school holiday period when it became customary for many of their supporters to take their vacations at the south coast to coincide with the cricket. Len Hutton made the highest score by a visiting batsman when he recorded 270 not out in 1947. Dick Moore made Hampshire's highest score at Dean Park – 316 against Warwickshire in 1937. Unsurprisingly, Phil Mead scored the most runs (5,961), though Roy Marshall hit the most centuries (16). Paul Terry and Tony Middleton shared the highest partnership when they put on 292 for the first wicket against Northamptonshire in 1990. Nevertheless, Dean Park was not generally a ground for tall scores. Kent made the highest innings total of 610 in 1906. They defeated Hampshire by an innings, claiming their first championship title in the process. Glamorgan also secured their first championship there in 1948. The wicket was usually a slow turner, upon which spin bowlers held sway.

Jack Newman and the Indian Srinivasan Venkataraghavan, both off-break bowlers, took nine wickets in an innings (9-131 in 1921 and 9-93 in 1971 respectively). The best match figures were by Derek Shackleton; 14-99 (7-67 and 7-32) against Warwickshire in Peter Sainsbury's benefit match in 1965. In the second innings, he took 6-12 in 11.3 overs in two spells from the sea end of the ground. Alec Kennedy claimed the most wickets (350). Uniquely for him, the engaging Colin Ingleby-Mackenzie earned notoriety in 1965 with a declaration in a rain-interrupted encounter against Worcestershire. He closed Hampshire's innings 147 runs behind after avoiding the follow-on just before lunch on the final day. Visiting captain Don Kenyon then declared after one ball. As the sun increased in intensity, the wicket became an old-fashioned 'sticky' and became unplayable. Hampshire were shot out for only 31, the lowest total at the ground, in just over an hour to leave Worcestershire winners by 115 runs. It was a significant factor in the visitors winning their second successive championship. Unseasonal rain in the Solent deprived Hampshire of a second successive championship in 1974, when the match against Yorkshire was abandoned without a ball being bowled. The elements also deprived Hampshire a win in their last match at Dean Park against Middlesex in 1992. The 22 overs lost to rain on the final morning were to prove crucial as Middlesex, following on, finished 75 runs ahead with nine wickets down. One-day matches were memorable for Hampshire's first ever limited-overs game – against Derbyshire in 1963 – and for

BOURNEMOUTH PAVILION DURING THE LAST MATCH THERE IN 1992

three televised virtuoso batting displays by Barry Richards in the early 1970s, as he hit hundreds against Kent, Lancashire and Leicestershire. The former innings of 132 not out remained the highest individual score in List A matches at the ground. Dean Park is still used by Dorset for Minor Counties matches and Hampshire made a nostalgic return there for a NatWest Trophy match in 1998. Hampshire played 336 first-class matches at Dean Park, winning 92, losing 117 and drawing 126. One match, against Lancashire in 1947, was tied.

BEST BOWLING FIGURES IN AN INNINGS

Hampshire's best bowling figures were recorded by Bob Cottam, who took 9-25 against Lancashire at Old Trafford in 1965. He dismissed the last nine batsmen at a personal cost of 15 runs in 55 balls.

BOWLING – MOST WICKETS FOR HAMPSHIRE

2,669	D. Shackleton
2,549	A.S. Kennedy
1,946	J.A. Newman
1,415	G.S. Boyes
1,245	P.J. Sainsbury
1,097	D.W. White
1,041	O.W. Herman
834	V.H.D. Cannings
826	M.D. Marshall
711	C.B. Llewellyn
708	S.D. Udal
693	R.M.H. Cottam
647	C.J. Knott
617	G. Hill
614	C.A. Connor
602	G. Brown
580	H. Baldwin
527	M. Heath
504	R.J. Maru

The most wickets taken by current players are 450 by Dimitri Mascarenhas and 299 by James Tomlinson.

WICKET WITH FIRST BALL IN FIRST-CLASS CRICKET

Three Hampshire bowlers have taken a wicket with their first ball in first-class cricket: Jon Ayling v Oxford University at The Parks in 1988, Chris Tremlett v New Zealand at Portsmouth in 2000, and James Schofield v Australians at the Rose Bowl in 2001. The latter was Schofield's only match for Hampshire.

BOWLING – WICKET-TAKING MONOPOLIES

In 1895, Hampshire's first season in the County Championship, Harry Baldwin (102 wickets) and Tom Soar (89) took 73.5 per cent of all the opposition wickets; a record for Hampshire. If James Wootton (37) is added to the equation, then the trio claimed 87.7 per cent of all the wickets to fall. However, the latter figure was exceeded in 1922. In that summer, Alec Kennedy (177), Jack Newman (121) and Stuart Boyes (94) captured a staggering 93.1 per cent of opposition wickets.

TEN WICKETS IN AN INNINGS FOR HAMPSHIRE

No man has ever taken ten wickets in an innings for the county. However, Hampshire's Alec Kennedy took 10-37 for the Players v Gentlemen at The Oval in 1927. Also, the South African Steve Jefferies claimed 10-59 for Western Province against Orange Free State at Newlands, Cape Town, in December 1987. He was not a Hampshire player at the time but made his debut for the county in April 1988.

TEN WICKETS IN AN INNINGS AGAINST HAMPSHIRE

Two men have performed the above feat. William Hickton took 10-46 for Lancashire at Old Trafford in the inaugural fixture between the two counties in 1870. The West Indian all-rounder Ottis Gibson repeated the achievement with 10-47 for Durham at Chester-le-Street in 2007.

NINE WICKETS IN AN INNINGS FOR HAMPSHIRE

Besides Bob Cottam, eight other bowlers have taken nine wickets in an innings for Hampshire: Derek Shackleton (4 times), Alec Kennedy (3), and Giles Baring, Stuart Boyes, Cardigan Connor, Alan Mullally, Jack Newman and David White once each.

NINE WICKETS IN AN INNINGS AND ON THE LOSING SIDE

Almost unbelievably, the first four men to take nine wickets in an innings for Hampshire all finished on the losing side.

Alec Kennedy: 9-33 v Lancashire at Liverpool, 1920
Lost by one run. Hampshire required only 66 to win but were bowled out for 64, losing their last five wickets for ten runs.
Jack Newman: 9-131 v Essex at Bournemouth, 1921
Lost by an innings and 55 runs.

Alec Kennedy: 9-46 v Derbyshire at Portsmouth, 1929
Lost by five wickets. Kennedy's match figures were 13-100.

Giles Baring: 9-26 v Essex at Colchester, 1931
Lost by two wickets.

Stuart Boyes finally laid the bogey at Yeovil in 1938. His 9-57 opened the way for a Hampshire victory by five wickets.

SEVENTEEN WICKETS AND ON THE LOSING SIDE

Two men have taken 17 wickets in a match against Hampshire yet finished on the losing side on both occasions. In 1876, Derbyshire's William Mycroft returned figures of 9-25 and 8-78 at the Antelope Ground, Southampton, but Hampshire eased home by one wicket. In 1895, Essex's Walter Mead took 8-67 and 9-52 at Northlands Road. On that occasion, Hampshire recorded an emphatic victory by 171 runs.

BEST MATCH FIGURES

Hampshire's best match figures were recorded by Jack Newman. He took 16-88 (8-65 and 8-23) against Somerset at Weston-super-Mare in 1927. In the course of both innings, he dismissed all of the Somerset batsmen.

MOST RUNS CONCEDED IN AN INNINGS

Two Hampshire bowlers have conceded more than 200 runs in an innings: Shaun Udal (213 v Surrey at The Oval in 2002); and Alec Kennedy (202 v Middlesex at Lord's in 1919). Hampshire fielded a depleted bowling attack on both occasions. In the latter match, Middlesex totalled 608/7 declared, Kennedy having taken all of the wickets.

MOST BALLS BOWLED IN AN INNINGS

In an incredibly boring match with Nottinghamshire at Southampton in 1934, both sides batted only once as they vied for first innings points. Nottinghamshire eventually prevailed as they headed Hampshire's first innings 494 by one run for the loss of eight wickets. Stuart Boyes bowled 80 overs, totalling 480 balls, a Hampshire record. In Hampshire's innings, the Nottinghamshire wicketkeeper, Lilley, had to be replaced because of the effects of an insect bite.

MOST RUNS CONCEDED IN A MATCH

In Hampshire's match against Somerset at the Rose Bowl in 2009, Imran Tahir took 7-140 and 2-120. His first innings effort enabled Hampshire to enforce the follow-on, but the county were unable to press for victory and the match finished as a tame draw. The 260 runs conceded by Tahir in the match constituted a Hampshire record.

MOST BALLS BOWLED IN A MATCH

In Hampshire's championship season of 1961, their match against Surrey was dominated by spin. The slow left-arm spinner from Gosport, Alan Wassell, made the crucial contribution to the county's eventual 58-run victory with figures of 56-28-76-5 and 37.3-13-87-7. The 561 balls he bowled in the match created a new Hampshire record, which still stands.

MOST WICKETS IN A SEASON

The greatest number of wickets taken by a Hampshire bowler in a season is 190 by Alec Kennedy in 1922. He also claimed five wickets in an innings on 20 occasions during the summer, another record. Both of those records are bound to stand in perpetuity. The last Hampshire bowler to take 100 wickets in a season was Malcolm Marshall (100 in 1986). Since the introduction of the four-day championship in 1993, the most number of wickets by a bowler is 74 by Shaun Udal that year, followed by Cardigan Connor's 72 in 1994, and Shane Warne's 70 in 2000. Shaun Udal has managed 50 wickets in a season six times since 1993, with Shane Warne doing so four times, Cardigan Connor, Alex Morris and James Tomlinson twice, and once each for David Balcombe, Peter Hartley, Dimitri Mascarenhas, Nixon McLean, Alan Mullally, Heath Streak and Imran Tahir.

BOWLING UNCHANGED THROUGH BOTH COMPLETED INNINGS

A pair of bowlers operating unchanged through a match was always a rarity. There have been only six instances in Hampshire's history. They usually occurred when there was a sub-standard pitch giving bowlers extravagant assistance. The last such occurrence was at Burton-on-Trent in 1958.

MERVYN BURDEN

Hampshire's off-spin bowler of the floppy hair and toothy grin from 1953 to 1963 was regarded as one of the county's great characters. He had no illusions about his batting prowess. When facing Frank Tyson, arguably the fastest bowler ever, he surveyed a well populated close field on the leg side. It prompted him to ask the fielders to spread out and leave enough room for himself!

MICHAEL CARBERRY

A Hampshire sage, steeped in cricket, once remarked that it was unusual for a man to be released by one county and enjoy sustained success with another. If it did occur, then there were special circumstances. Michael Carberry is a man who has vindicated that view, the only exception being that he found fulfilment with a third county. He played consistently for both Surrey and Kent beforehand, but finding his way barred at both, he joined Hampshire in 2006 and has been outstanding since. His 22 first-class centuries are a record for any batsman in the Ageas Bowl era. His sheer weight of runs has seen him rewarded with two overseas tours to Bangladesh and others to Australia and India with various England sides. Carberry also scored a century for England Lions against New Zealand at the Rose Bowl in 2008. Towards the end of 2010, a life-threatening condition, blood clots on his lungs, was then discovered just prior to the England Lions tour to the West Indies. He did not play again until July 2011. In only his third match after his return, he gave an emphatic reminder of his international credentials with an innings of 300 not out in 510 minutes against Yorkshire at the Rose Bowl. He and Neil Mackenzie (237) completed an epic third-wicket partnership of 523 in 475 minutes, a record for the County Championship. Carberry is an imposing figure at the crease. Shaven-headed, and resembling a left-handed Viv Richards in build and gait, he drives powerfully and cuts, pulls and hooks with relish. He is particularly adept at building an innings. In 2009 he scored four centuries in successive matches. Two years earlier he had made a century in each innings against Worcestershire at Kidderminster. In the last two summers, he suddenly became the most explosive batsman in the country in limited-overs cricket. His extraordinary innings (68 off just 36 balls with five sixes) on a slow, sluggish pitch at Hove was the main contributory factor to Hampshire reaching the CB final at Lord's in 2012. He posted an opening partnership of 129 in just 12.4 overs with James Vince (58). His fielding in both the Twenty20 and CB finals in that year was electric. Carberry's appearance on the cricket field is certainly an occasion to be relished.

FASTEST TO 100 CAREER WICKETS

Those Hampshire bowlers who have taken their first 100 wickets for the county in 20 matches or less have been:

Harry Baldwin	15
Charles Llewellyn	16
Tom Soar	19
Andy Roberts	20
Alan Mullally	20

Remarkably, Baldwin made his first-class debut for the county in 1877, when he was wicketless. On his return to first-class cricket in 1895, when he was aged 34, he reached the landmark in 14 further matches.

BROTHERS WHO HAVE PLAYED FOR HAMPSHIRE

F.T.A.H. Bathurst and L.H. Bathurst; F.W.D. Quinton and J.M. Quinton; G.N. Bignell and H.G. Bignell; A.B. Ridley and A.W. Ridley; D.E. Blake and J.P. Blake; J.S. Rutherford and A.P. Rutherford; A.C. Cecil and E.D.C. Cecil; C.L. Smith and R.A. Smith; A.J. Duncan and D.W.J. Duncan; G.J. Spencer-Smith and O. Spencer-Smith (twins); E.L. Ede and G.M. Ede (twins); A.E. Evans and D.M. Evans; Sir H. Stewart and W.A. Stewart; A.J. Evans and R. du B. Evans; H.W. Studd and R.A. Studd; S.G. Francis and J.F. Francis; F. Tate and H.W. Tate; A.A. Henley and R. Henley; C.E. Ward and H.F. Ward; E.E. Light and W.F. Light; A.C. Morris and Z.C. Morris.

C.S.C. Bowen and E.E. Bowen, and W. Ridding and C.H. Ridding also played for Hampshire but neither of the first named did so in first-class cricket. The Ede brothers are the only twins to play in the same match for Hampshire. They did so on 13 occasions between 1864-1869.

HEAT HAZE STOPPED PLAY

Play was held up for a short time on the second day of Hampshire's match against Glamorgan at Swansea in 1946 due to a heat haze which enshrouded the ground.

INELIGIBLE PLAYER

In 1909, George Wilder, who played for Sussex in 1905 and 1906, took the field for Hampshire against Derbyshire at Southampton. However, it was ruled that he was not properly qualified and he did not appear for the county again.

GEORGE BROWN

In terms of his sheer versatility, George Brown was one of cricket's finest all-rounders. He was born in Cowley, Oxford, on 6 October 1887. Tall, with high cheekbones and a ruddy complexion, he made his Hampshire debut in 1908. A left-handed batsman, he scored 22,962 runs (average 26.88), including 37 centuries, took 602 wickets (average 29.66) as a right-arm bowler, held 484 catches and stumped 51 batsmen. He was, in fact, rarely Hampshire's regular wicketkeeper, Jimmy Stone and Walter Livsey holding that post. Yet he was chosen for England in 1921 and MCCs tour of South Africa in 1922/23 as the first-choice wicketkeeper. He was also selected in that capacity for the pivotal Ashes Test at the Oval in 1926, but a damaged finger forced his withdrawal. In his early years, he was described as the 'furthest thrower in the game'. He was a brilliant fielder at mid-off and the bravest and most excellent of close-to-the-wicket fielders, especially at silly point or short leg. As a bowler, he started life as being just short of genuinely fast. In his later years, he bowled at about Derek Shackleton's pace. In the match against Northamptonshire at Southampton in 1927, he batted, bowled, fielded and kept wicket. Brown was one of the most gifted players of fast bowling that ever bestrode the batting crease. When Australia's fast bowlers, Jack Gregory and Ted McDonald, were laying waste to England's batsmen in 1921, the selectors called up Brown. He scored 57, 46, 31, 32 and 84 to finish second in England's batting averages. He was always at his best in a fight. The greater the challenge, the more magnificent was his response. He scored two double centuries against Yorkshire, including his career best 232 not out at Leeds in 1920, and 106 not out against county champions Lancashire at the age of 42 in 1930. Famously, it was his 172 at Edgbaston in 1922 that pulled the game out of the fire when Hampshire were in a hopeless position. Brown left the game in 1933. This colossus of a man suffered greatly after his playing days were over. His son died in a bombing raid over Southampton, his wife experienced a long period of illness and only his strong constitution enabled him to survive a succession of heart attacks. He died in Winchester on 3 December 1961. Fittingly, his ashes were scattered over the County Ground at Southampton.

GEORGE BROWN STORIES

The scattering of George Brown's ashes resulted in an interesting postscript. Early on in the following season, Roy Marshall was caught behind off a ball that moved disconcertingly. He always claimed that it pitched on Brown's remains.

'HE'S NOT FAST'

In 1913, when Kent played at Portsmouth they remembered that Brown tickled the ribs of a few of their batsmen with his quick bowling in a previous match. One of their players told him that Kent's own fast bowler, Arthur Fielder, would retort in kind. After opener Jimmy Stone retired hurt, Fielder bowled a short ball to Brown almost as soon as he reached the wicket. He dropped his bat and deliberately took the ball full on the chest and exclaimed 'he's not fast'. He went on to make 71. About 20 years later, he adopted the same ploy when facing Bill Voce of Nottinghamshire at Bournemouth. He was now older and the body less robust. After taking the ball on the chest, he swayed and sank to his knees just as he emitted 'fast'.

THE BROWN SCOOP

Brown was quick to anger. After his captain Lionel Tennyson relegated him to number ten against Warwickshire at Southampton in 1925, he displayed his annoyance by going to the wicket with an old bat from the groundsman's hut. He immediately rolled out the Brownscoop, a forerunner of the Dilscoop now used regularly in Twenty20s. He hit a ball from fast bowler Harry Howell over the wicketkeeper's head and the sightscreen for six. His bat then split after another forceful shot. Rather than call for a replacement, he tore the blade in two, handed one part to the umpire and continued to bat with the other portion. He made 17. It must be said that Hampshire were in a comfortable position when Brown walked to the wicket and won by an innings.

BROWN THE UMPIRE

After Brown's playing days were over, he umpired in 1935 and 1936. It seems he possessed a trigger finger, answering almost every appeal in the affirmative. It was said that he was the only umpire to complete 100 dismissals in May.

HAMPSHIRE'S CAPTAINS

1864–1869	G.M. Ede
1875–1878	C. Booth
1879	R.H. Wood
1880–1882	H.W.R. Bencraft
1883–1885	A.H. Wood
1895	H.W.R. Bencraft
1896–1899	E.G. Wynyard
1900–1902	C. Robson
1903–1914	E.M. Sprot
1919–1933	Hon L.H. (Lord) Tennyson
1934–1935	W.G.L.F. Lowndes
1936–1937	R.H. Moore
1938	C.G.A. Paris
1939	G.R. Taylor
1946–1957	E.D.R. Eagar
1958–1965	A.C.D. Ingleby-Mackenzie
1966–1970	R.E. Marshall
1971–1978	R.M.C. Gilliat
1979	G.R. Stephenson
1980–1984	N.E.J. Pocock
1985–1995	M.C.J. Nicholas
1996–1997	J.P. Stephenson
1998–2002	R.A. Smith
2003	J.P. Crawley
2004–2007	S.K. Warne
2008–2010	A.D. Mascarenhas
2011	D.G. Cork
2012–2013	J.H.K. Adams

MOST APPEARANCES AS CAPTAIN

Lionel Tennyson made most appearances a captain (323), followed by Desmond Eagar (310), Mark Nicholas (247), Colin Ingleby-Mackenzie (244), E.M. Sprot (213), Richard Gilliat (160), Roy Marshall (156) and Nick Pocock (100). Since 1993, Robin Smith has captained Hampshire on most occasions (88).

SEVEN CAPTAINS IN THE SEASON

Though Lionel (Lord) Tennyson was the appointed Hampshire captain in 1933, he was available for only four matches that season. The county were led by six other captains during the summer: C.P. Mead, A.K. Judd, G.L.O. Jessop, J.P. Parker, G. Brown and A.S. Kennedy.

CAPTAINED HAMPSHIRE ON FIRST-CLASS DEBUT

Two men have captained the county in their initial appearance in first-class cricket. G.M. Ede skippered Hampshire in their inaugural match in first-class cricket against Sussex at The Antelope Ground in 1864. A.H. Wood took up the reins on his debut when the county played Lancashire at Old Trafford in 1870. Also, both Desmond Eagar and John Stephenson led Hampshire on their debuts for the county, but they had previously played for Gloucestershire and Essex respectively.

CAPTAINS MISCELLANY

Most runs: 11,781 ....Lionel Tennyson
Most centuries: 21 ....Mark Nicholas
Highest score: 316 ....Dick Moore
Most wickets: 206... Shane Warne
Best bowling figures: 8-26........... Charles Knott v Cambridge University
at Bournemouth, 1937

DID NOT BAT OR BOWL (1)

Three men have played for Hampshire who, in their only appearance, neither batted nor bowled. The first was C.R. Gunner at Derby in 1878. Rain only permitted play on the first day, and a small part of the second, during which Hampshire made 74-7 in reply to Derbyshire's 137. Gunner, a 25-year-old amateur from Bishop's Waltham, was due to bat at the fall of the eighth wicket. He did leave a mark on the match, though, by holding a catch in the Derbyshire innings. His son J.H. played for Hampshire in six matches from 1906–07, and was killed in the First World War (see Roll of Honour).

DID NOT BAT OR BOWL (2)

Oswald Wykeham Cornwallis's only match was cruelly cut short at lunch on the first day of Hampshire's game against Kent at Southampton in 1921. Both he and his brother, Wykeham Stanley Cornwallis, who was in the Kent side, withdrew from the fixture when they received news that their oldest brother, Captain Fiennes Wykeham Mann Cornwallis, had been shot dead the previous evening in an IRA terrorist atrocity in Ireland. Oswald had not batted in the pre-lunch session. Both brothers were recorded as being 'absent' on the official scorecard.

DID NOT BAT OR BOWL (3)

Not many cricketers could have experienced such a short career in the first-class game as Frederick James Hyland, a right-arm medium pace bowler from the Ringwood area. He was a 30-year-old trialist who was called upon to play at Northampton in June 1924, due to a catalogue of injuries. It was a wet summer and he had to wait until 5.45pm on the first day to take the field. Only two overs were bowled before the rain returned, after which the conditions prevented any more play in the match. It is not known if Hyland even fielded the ball. Hyland later played in Norfolk and Scotland before earning a reputation as a trophy-winning nurseryman in Cheshire. He died in 1964.

DESMOND EAGAR

Desmond Eagar was the beating heart of Hampshire CCC from 1946 until his sudden death while on holiday in Devon in September 1977. He made his debut for Gloucestershire while still at school in 1935 and played for the side until the Second World War. He also gained an Oxford Blue in 1939. After service with the South Wales Borderers during the war, he was appointed captain and joint secretary of Hampshire in 1946 and secretary in 1955. He gave priority to improving Hampshire's fielding, allied to filtering younger players into an ageing side. It was this strategy, in tandem with shrewd signings, that took the county to third place in the County Championship in 1955, the highest position they had yet achieved. He handed over the side to Colin Ingleby-Mackenzie in 1958, after the pair had shared the captaincy in the previous years. With the support of Harry Altham, Arthur Holt and Eagar behind the scenes, Hampshire progressed to their first championship in 1961. Though his batting never quite realised its full potential, his close-to-the-wicket fielding was outstanding as exemplified by 333 catches in 311 matches. Off the field, he guided the county's affairs with discretion and skill. These assets were recognised when he was chosen as assistant manager for the MCC tour of Australia in 1958/59. He was a notable collector of cricket memorabilia; upon his death the sale of his antiquarian books and pamphlets raised a record £717,515 at Christie's. He was one of the joint authors of *Hampshire County Cricket* (the official history published in 1957) and edited the *Hampshire Handbook* from 1955–1977.

CAPTAINED IN THREE TIED MATCHES

Desmond Eagar holds the unusual record of being the only man for any county to be involved in three tied championship matches: v Lancashire at Bournemouth in 1947, v Kent at Southampton in 1950, and v Sussex at Eastbourne in 1955. Moreover, he was captain in all three matches.

IN THE BEGINNING

The first two references to cricket in Hampshire both originate from Winchester College. A Latin poem, written in 1647, alludes to the game being played by pupils on St. Catherine's Hill, Winchester. A biography of Bishop Ken, a leading 17th century cleric, also mentions that he played cricket as a boy at the school, which he attended from 1652 to 1655.

FIRST REFERENCE TO HAMPSHIRE CRICKETERS

The first definite reference to Hampshire cricketers taking part in a major match dates from August 1729 when Kent hosted a combined Sussex, Surrey and Hampshire side in Penshurst Park. The report quaintly states, 'The latter got (within three) in one hand, as the former did in two hands, so the Kentish men threw it up.' The match is generally regarded as the first victory by an innings. Unfortunately, the names of the participating Hampshire players are lost to history. The match was played for the considerable sum of 100 guineas.

EARLIEST MATCH IN HAMPSHIRE

The first reference to a specific match being played in the county dates from May 1733. It was at Stubbington, near Fareham between the Bachelors and Married Men. The same sides played each other again at Titchfield a week later. The Married Men won both encounters, much to the chagrin of their younger opponents.

HAMPSHIRE'S FIRST MATCH

The earliest reference to Hampshire as a county team originates from a match against Sussex, believed to be at Goodwood, in June 1766. The game was played at the time when Hampshire, under the patronage of the well-heeled Hambledon Club, were becoming cricket's major power. However, like the match in 1729, the composition of the teams is unknown. Hampshire won the match.

RUNNERS-UP (1)

County Championship table 1958:

	P	W	D	L	Bonus	Pts
Surrey	28	14	5	8	32	212
Hampshire	28	12	6	10	28	186
Somerset	28	12	9	7	20	174

Hampshire continued their drive to the title by achieving their highest place since their admission to the County Championship in 1895. Under the flamboyant leadership of Colin Ingleby-Mackenzie in his first season as captain, the county headed the table for eight glorious weeks from 27 June until 26 August before Surrey, who won the last of their seven successive championship titles, pulled away. From 21 May until 12 August only one match, against Middlesex at Lord's, was lost. The county were nip and tuck with Surrey throughout the season. However, the challenge hit the buffers terminally in an extraordinary match against Derbyshire at Burton-on-Trent in mid-August when the county were dismissed for 23 and 55. Thirty-nine wickets fell on the second day. Derek Shackleton and Malcolm Heath bowled unchanged throughout; Mike Barnard top-scored in both innings, with five (jointly with Henry Horton) and 16. The Hampshire players described the pitch as a whist drive wicket. They did not know whether to play high or to play low. Hampshire, though, were traumatised. Ingleby-Mackenzie described the experience as the most shattering of his career.

Though the county won the following match against Essex at Clacton-on-Sea, their batting never recovered its former buoyancy and they were unable to register a win in their last four matches. Rain also did not help Hampshire's cause, as did Ingleby-Mackenzie's luck with the toss. The county lost over 100 hours to the weather while the captain lost 18 of the last 22 flips of the coin. Hampshire's achievement in running the formidable Surrey team so close was therefore outstanding. Roy Marshall again headed the batting averages (1,627 runs, averaging 36.97) and the phenomenal Derek Shackleton harvested a career best 161 wickets (average 15.33) in the championship, the most by any bowler in the competition. The young captain twice gave notice of his fast scoring prowess with his left-handed batting by clouting centuries in less than even time. He flew to his hundred against Somerset at Bournemouth in only 61 minutes, the fastest century of the season. He had attended Royal Ascot on the previous day and only took to his bed after dawn had broken. Thankfully for him, he won the toss and slept most of the day in the changing room before going in to bat. He won the match against Kent at Southampton by reaching the landmark in 98 minutes.

FASTEST CENTURY OF THE SEASON

Hampshire players have scored the fastest century for the season on six occasions:

1911.........E.M. Sprot v Gloucestershire at Bristol (45 minutes)
1927.........Lionel Tennyson v Gloucestershire at Southampton
           (55 minutes)
1957.........Roy Marshall v Kent at Southampton (66 minutes)
1958.........Colin Ingleby-Mackenzie v Somerset at Bournemouth
           (61 minutes)
1965.........Roy Marshall v Oxford University at The Parks (102 minutes)
1978.........Gordon Greenidge v Glamorgan at Southampton (82
           minutes)

Sprot's hundred remains the fastest scored by a Hampshire player.

PLAYED WITH THE BAT'S EDGE

How good was Barry Richards? His contemporaries often tell the story of net sessions in which he would play the bowling with the edge of the bat and that he rarely missed 'middling' the ball.

FIELDED IN CIVVIES

The Nottinghamshire players fielded in lounge suits on the third morning of their match at Southampton in 1930. The umpires had allowed an extra half-hour's play on the previous evening in expectation of a result. However, at 7pm and with the scores level, the umpires called 'time'. Alec Kennedy, wearing whites, hit the second ball of the morning's play to the boundary, thereby sealing the county's third win against the then-county champions. A photograph of the event hangs in the Ageas Bowl pavilion.

MOST MATCHES WITHOUT RECEIVING CAP

Alan Castell has the unwanted record of playing the most matches for the county without receiving his county cap: 110. He started his career as a 17-year-old in 1971, as a promising leg-spin bowler whom Bill Alley of Somerset thought was better than Richie Benaud at the same age. However, frustrated at his restricted opportunities, he changed to bowling seamers from 1966. He left the club in 1971. Richard Lewis, who had the unenviable task of understudying Barry Richards and Gordon Greenidge for virtually all his career, is next in the same category. He appeared in 103 matches without winning his cap.

THE CRICKETING DUKE

The Duke of Edinburgh took his own team to play Hampshire in a one-day friendly at Bournemouth in 1949, in aid of the National Playing Fields Association. His side won a close affair by one wicket. He dismissed Gerry Dawson with his right-arm medium bowling, and then scored 12, twice unfurling classical off-drives to send the ball to the boundary. An XI under his name also appeared at Southampton in 1954, but he did not play in the match.

MARSHALL AND GRAY

Roy Marshall and Jimmy Gray were Hampshire's most prolific opening partnership. Between 1955 and 1962, they started the county's innings with a century stand on 33 occasions. Four of these came in five successive matches in the last of those years. In the intervening game, they had put on 90. Hampshire lost only three matches in which they opened with a century partnership.

INAUGURAL FIRST-CLASS MATCH

Hampshire started their inaugural match as a first-class county against Sussex at the Antelope Ground, Southampton, on 7 July 1864, with only ten men. G.H. Case, a doctor, was absent throughout their first innings, which realised only 63. Case opened second time around, top scoring with 48 out of 122. The county lost by ten wickets in two days.

HAMPSHIRE'S DOCTORS

Besides Case (see above), eight other men played for Hampshire in first-class cricket who were either doctors at the time, or went on to qualify afterwards: Russell Bencraft, E.P.G. Causton, T.C. Fox, A.A. Henley, G. Mannings, R.H. Mornement, B.G. von Melle and H.E. Webb.

SIR RUSSELL BENCRAFT

Sir Russell Bencraft was born in the Southampton Workhouse, where his father was the medical officer. No man did more towards advancing Hampshire cricket in its formative years. He was treasurer from 1880–1893, supervised the move from the Antelope Ground to the new County Ground at Northlands Road in 1885, was honorary secretary when Hampshire regained first-class status in 1895, was chairman from 1919–1934 and finally president. A doctor by profession (see above), Sir Russell was one of the most prominent dignitaries in the civic affairs of

Southampton for some 50 years. He was also on the MCC committee and first president of the Southern Football League. He served as president of Southampton St. Mary's FC, the first incarnation of Southampton FC. When he was knighted in 1924, over 400 sportsmen attended a dinner in his honour. An even greater number assembled to celebrate his 60 years of service to Hampshire in 1937. Sir Russell played in 44 matches for Hampshire between 1876 and 1896. His contributions were modest, though he scored 195 against Warwickshire in 1889 when the county were not regarded as a first-class county. As a medical student, he once scored six centuries in a week. He was forced to move from his house in Southampton during the Second World War when it was destroyed by German bombs. He died at Compton, near Winchester, on Christmas Day in 1943, six months after his left leg was amputated above the knee.

FIRST TO TARGETS

The following Hampshire players have been the first men in the country to reach cricket's landmark targets in the following years:

1,000 runs: 1914 Phil Mead (14 June); 1985 Chris Smith (17 June); 1992 Tony Middleton (17 June)

100 wickets: 1914 Alec Kennedy (10 July); 1962 Derek Shackleton (11 July); 1964 Derek Shackleton (1 August); 1968 Bob Cottam (27 July); 1974 Andy Roberts (17 August); 1982 Malcolm Marshall (25 August)

1,000 runs and 100 wickets: 1926 Jack Newman (31 July); 1948 Jim Bailey (10 August).

THE GALLOPING MAJOR

In 1899, R.M. Poore achieved his first 1,000 runs in only 11 innings, easily a Hampshire record. He managed this in 38 days between 14 June and 21 July. During his summer's cricket, which finished on 12 August, he hit (that being the operative word) 1,551 runs at an average of 91.23. His Hampshire average was an eye-watering 116. His 21 innings realised seven centuries and three fifties, and he headed the country's batting averages for the season. The Somerset bowlers must have been in awe of him. He started his incredible sequence on 14 June with 104 and 119 not out against them at Portsmouth, becoming the first Hampshire player to score a century in each innings. He remained the only batsman to do so at Portsmouth. In the return at Taunton, he struck 304 not out in 410 minutes. In that match, he and his fellow soldier, Captain E.G. Wynyard (225 not out), added 411 in 260 minutes for the sixth wicket. Long after his playing days were over, he was once asked how he would tackle Harold Larwood, England's legendary fast bowler of the inter-war years. His reply was, 'Gad, sir, I'd give him the charge.'

FIRST CENTURY IN CHAMPIONSHIP CRICKET

Hampshire's first century in the County Championship was by another soldier, Captain F.W.D. Quinton. He hit 178 in only 195 minutes against Leicestershire at Grace Road, Leicester, in 1895. Quinton was a hard-hitting right-handed batsman. His potential force as a county batsman was also demonstrated in 1896 when he struck five consecutive fifties in championship matches. Unfortunately, as with many of Hampshire's soldiers who played prior to the First World War, service commitments restricted his appearances.

MOST CATCHES IN CAREER FOR HAMPSHIRE

633	C.P. Mead
601	P.J. Sainsbury
484	A.S. Kennedy
471	G.S. Boyes
375	G. Brown
333	E.D.R. Eagar
328	V.P. Terry
315	C.G. Greenidge
313	H.M. Barnard

Barry Richards held 264 catches in 204 matches. His average of 1.29 catches per match is a Hampshire record. It is interesting to note that Mead, Sainsbury and Boyes were all slow left-arm bowlers, as is Liam Dawson (see below). The most catches held by a current player is 124 by Jimmy Adams.

MOST CATCHES IN AN INNINGS

Five players have held five catches in an innings: F.W.D. Quinton, Phil Mead, Barry Richards, Nick Pocock and Paul Terry.

MOST CATCHES IN A MATCH

Three men have held seven catches in a match: Tom Dean, Raj Maru and Liam Dawson.

MOST CATCHES IN A SEASON

Peter Sainsbury holds the record with 56 in 1957. The most since 1993, when the four-day County Championship was introduced, is 37 in 17 matches by Liam Dawson in 2012. The latter's average of 2.18 catches per match in the summer created a new Hampshire record.

PLAYED IN FOUR DECADES

Eight men have played for Hampshire in four decades: John Arnold (1919–50), Jim Bailey (1927–52), George Brown (1908–33), E.I.M. Barrett (1896–1925), Leo Harrison (1939–66), Alec Kennedy (1907–36), Phil Mead (1905–36) and Jack Newman (1906–30). Harry Baldwin's career (1877–1905) spanned four decades but he did not play first-class cricket for the county in the 1880s.

THE OXFORD CONNECTION

From 1902 to 1972, there was virtually an unbroken line of Oxford-born cricketers who gave wonderful service to the county. Chief among them were Alec Bowell (1902–27), George Brown (1908–33), John Arnold (1929–50), Lofty Herman (1929–48), Neville Rogers (1946–55) and Alan Castell (1961–71).

MOST FIRST-CLASS CENTURIES FOR HAMPSHIRE

138	C.P. Mead
60	R.E. Marshall
49	R.A. Smith
48	C.G. Greenidge
41	C.L. Smith
38	B.A. Richards
37	V.P. Terry, G. Brown
36	J. Arnold
34	M.C.J. Nicholas
32	H. Horton
30	J.R. Gray
27	D.R. Turner
26	T.E. Jesty, N.H. Rogers
25	H.A.W. Bowell

The most centuries scored by current players are 22 by Michael Carberry and 17 by Jimmy Adams.

MOST CENTURIES IN A SEASON

Philip Mead established Hampshire's record with 12 centuries in 1928. The most by a batsman since 1993 is six by John Crawley in 2006.

MOST DOUBLE CENTURIES FOR THE COUNTY

Phil Mead scored 11 double centuries for the county. Gordon Greenidge (six), and Jimmy Adams (four) are the next on the list. George Brown, John Crawley and Roy Marshall all made three, though Crawley's tally includes two triple centuries.

MOST CENTURIES AGAINST HAMPSHIRE

The great Jack Hobbs scored the most centuries against Hampshire (11), followed by Kent's Frank Woolley and Warwickshire's W.G. Quaife, both ten. Interestingly, all but one of Quaife's hundreds were made on a Warwickshire ground.

CENTURY WITHOUT A BOUNDARY

Arthur Ridley was regarded as one of the best all-round cricketers of the 1870s. He gave credence to that view when he set about Kent at Faversham. First he held the Hampshire innings together with 104 in an all-out total of 277. His century was unique in that it did not contain a single boundary. He then confused Kent with his right-arm lobs to the extent of 5-52 and 5-61. He and Fred Tate (5-67) bowled unchanged in Kent's first innings of 129. After dismissing Kent for 142 (Tate 4-54), Hampshire won by an innings and six runs. The Newbury-born Ridley was able to play for the county only between 1875 and 1878. A director of a brewery firm, business interests subsequently necessitated a move to London, after which he turned out for Middlesex.

HAMPSHIRE'S ENGLAND CAPTAINS

Three Hampshire players, all batsmen, have captained England. C.B. Fry was the first to do so in the Triangular Tournament of 1912 in which England won four Tests and drew the other two to win the competition. Fry remains England's only unbeaten captain. Lionel Tennyson captained England in three Tests against Australia in 1921. His side, despite his heroic gallantry, lost his first Test in charge but then drew the final two to bring a sequence of eight successive defeats at the hands of the Aussies to a halt. Kevin Pietersen, still nominally a Hampshire player, captained England in one Test against South Africa at The Oval in 2008, scoring 100, and twice against India on the ensuing tour shortly afterwards, making 144 at Chennai. He was the first Hampshire player to score a century for England while captain and the first to captain England in an overseas Test. In Pietersen's three Tests as captain, England won his first in charge and then lost and drew the other two in India. Pietersen also captained England in five ODIs against South Africa (winning four and a no result) and five ODIs in India, all of which were lost. He is the only Hampshire player to skipper England in ODIs.

HAMPSHIRE PLAYERS IN THE FOOTBALL LEAGUE

Thirteen Hampshire players appeared in the Football League:

J. Arnold	Southampton	1929/30–32/33	111 appearances
	Fulham	1932/33–38/39	202
H.M. Barnard	Portsmouth	1953/54–58/59	116
A.K. Campbell	Southampton	1920/21–25/26	157
R. Dare	Exeter City	1950/51	6
E.J. Drake	Southampton	1931/32–33/34	72
	Arsenal	1933/34–38/39	168
B.R.S. Harrison	Crystal Palace	1955/56–58/59	92
	Southampton	1959/60	3
	Exeter City	1960/61	18
A.G. Holt	Southampton	1932/33–38/39	202
H. Horton	Blackburn Rovers	1946/47–50/51	92
	Southampton	1951/52–53/54	75
	Bradford P A	1954/55	27
A.E. Knight	Portsmouth	1920/21–21/22	34
L.V. Lodge	Birmingham City	1895/96	1
R.O. Prouton	Swindon Town	1952/53	13
D.P.N. Roper	Southampton	1946/47	40
	Arsenal	1947/48–56/57	297
	Southampton	1957/58–58/59	80
G.R. Stephenson	Derby County	1961/62–62/63	11
	Shrewsbury Town	1964/65	3
	Rochdale	1965/66–66/67	50

The football careers of all the above ran concurrently, either in part or fully, with their Hampshire appearances, with the exception of A.K. Campbell, L.V. Lodge, and Bob Stephenson.

HAMPSHIRE'S TEST CRICKETERS FOR ENGLAND

Twenty-eight Hampshire cricketers have played in Test matches for England, of whom 22 were with the county when they did so. The figures

in brackets give the number of Tests played when with Hampshire:
J. Arnold (1), G. Brown (7), M.A. Carberry (6), R.M.H. Cottam (2), J.P. Crawley (8), C.B. Fry (9), D.I. Gower (11), C. Heseltine (2), A.J.L. Hill (3), A.S. Kennedy (5), C.P. Mead (17), A.D. Mullally (1), K.P. Pietersen (66), D. Shackleton (7), C.L. Smith (8), R.A. Smith (62), L.H. Tennyson (9), V.P. Terry (2), C.T. Tremlett (3), S.D. Udal (4), D.W. White (2) and E.G. Wynyard (3).

Crawley (Lancashire), Fry (Sussex) and Gower (Leicestershire) had also played for England before joining Hampshire. Pietersen and Tremlett (both Surrey) went on to play in further Tests after leaving the county. A further five Hampshire players, D.G. Cork, N.G. Cowans, A.J. Evans, L.H. Gay and J.P. Stephenson, also appeared in Tests but were with other counties at the time. When V.A. Barton played in the first ever Test in South Africa in 1891/92, he was 'unattached'.

HAMPSHIRE PLAYERS IN AN FA CUP FINAL

Six Hampshire players have appeared in an FA Cup Final: E.E. Bowen (Wanderers 1872 and 1873), L. Bury (Old Etonians 1879), Ted Drake (Arsenal 1936), C.B. Fry (Southampton 1902), Don Roper (Arsenal 1952) and E.G. Wynyard (Old Carthusians 1881). Only Drake and Wynyard were current Hampshire players when they made their Cup Final appearance, and, coincidentally, both scored.

THREE HAMPSHIRE PLAYERS FOR SAINTS

On 21 January 1933 Johnnie Arnold, Ted Drake and Arthur Holt played for Southampton at Bury where they lost 1-0. It was the only time the three appeared together for the Saints.

PHILIP MEAD THE FOOTBALLER

In his early days with Hampshire Phil Mead was on the books of Southampton FC. He made his only appearance for the first team in the Southern League as a goalkeeper. As befitting an excellent slip fielder, he kept a clean sheet in a 0-0 draw against West Ham at The Dell.

FORMATION OF HAMPSHIRE CCC

After three abortive attempts, in 1795, 1839 and 1849, the dream of establishing a Hampshire County Cricket Club was realised in September 1863. The previous year, a group of gentlemen, headed by Sir Frederick Bathurst, a leading amateur cricketer in the 1850s, and Thomas Chamberlayne of Cranbury Park, Otterbourne, met with a view to reviving the county's cricket which had limped along for virtually the whole of the 19th century. In August 1863 a further meeting was held at The Antelope Inn, Southampton, 'for the purpose of making the preliminary arrangements for the formation of a County Cricket Club by means of which annual contests with Surrey, Sussex, etc. can be secured, and an organisation for fostering and encouraging the game of cricket'. At this meeting it was unanimously resolved that:

'1 It was desirable that a County Club for Hampshire be established.
2 Thomas Chamberlayne, Esq., be requested to become President of the Club.
3 Mr. E.L. Ede be requested to act as Secretary pro tem.
4 A Committee be appointed to prepare Rules and Regulations and to submit the same for approval to a General Meeting to be held at The Antelope Inn on Friday September 11, 1863.'

A regular committee of 19 were appointed. Mr G.M. Ede (E.L.'s brother) was appointed honorary secretary, John Hunt as hon treasurer and the Earls of Portsmouth and Uxbridge were invited to become vice-presidents. It was agreed that the Antelope Ground, rented on an annual basis, should be its headquarters and the yearly subscription for members should be one guinea. Members were enrolled, colts' matches were arranged, a marquee was bought, a club standard with the county arms was ordered and the president presented a horse for work on the ground.

THE REMARKABLE C.B. FRY

While at Sussex, between 1894 and 1908, Charles Burgess Fry established himself as one of the great English batsmen. However, his work with the Training Ship *Mercury* on the River Hamble had enabled him to qualify for Hampshire. He made his Hampshire debut in 1909 at the age of 37. Befitting a man who wrote arguably the classic treatise on batting, he then played with great distinction for the county until 1921 when he was 49 years of age. He scored 14 centuries for the county in only 44 matches. His average, 58.90, is by far the highest of any man appearing for Hampshire for any length of time. He played in nine Tests for England while with Hampshire and captained his country to victory in the rain-ruined 1912 Triangular Tournament, which also featured Australia and South Africa. He is the only man to captain England without losing a Test. He was again asked to lead his country in his last season. However, owing to injury and innate fears about being able to cope with the Australian fast bowling, he declined. He did recommend though that England select Lionel Tennyson as a batsman. The results were spectacular.

C.B. FRY (2)

John Arlott wrote that C.B. Fry was 'probably the most variously gifted Englishmen of any age'. His brain was such that he won an exhibition to Wadham College, Oxford, ahead of two future Lord Chancellors. He took a first in Classical Moderations and an even better fourth in Greats. At the end of his career he accompanied and wrote speeches for his great Sussex partner, K.S. Ranjitsinhji, at the League of Nations. And in 1921 he was offered the throne of Albania! He later became a thought-provoking sports journalist, author, poet, an accomplished writer of Latin and Greek, founder and editor of the outstanding *C.B. Fry's Magazine*.

C.B. FRY (3)

Fry once told his biographer, Denzil Batchelor, that he was tiring of cricket and was thinking of taking up horse-racing instead. Batchelor promptly enquired if he would be doing so as 'owner, trainer, jockey or horse?'

C.B. FRY (4)

The greatest of Fry's athletic feats occurred at Iffley Road, Oxford in 1893, when he equalled the world long jump record of 23ft 6.5ins. His performance was delivered in adverse circumstances. He had spiked his toe and was not sure he would be fit enough to jump. Also, due to a damaged take-off board he had to jump from some three to four inches behind it. His actual leap was therefore actually longer than his record. Legend has it that prior to his jump he put down his post-lunch cigar and then returned to finish it afterwards.

C.B. FRY (5)

When at Oxford, Fry won Blues in all four years for athletics, association football and cricket. He only missed a Blue for rugby because of an injury sustained just before the university match. He also played football for England while an under graduate and went on to play in the FA Cup Final for Southampton in 1902. He was the only amateur on either side. On the following Monday he scored 82 for London County against Surrey at The Oval. He was also a fine golfer, billiards and tennis player, fisherman and rifle shot.

C. B. FRY (6)

Fry's athletic powers remained with him into old age. John Arlott recalled that, at the age of 76, Fry 'swung himself athletically over a tottering ladder onto a wrecked landing of the commentary box at Old Trafford'. Peter West, a former BBC commentator, also recalled him ascending a staircase four steps at a time at the same age.

UNSUCCESSFUL POLITICIANS

C.B. Fry stood for Parliament three times as a candidate for the Liberal Party, between 1922 and 1924, at Brighton, Banbury and Oxford respectively. He was unsuccessful on each occasion. John Arlott also stood as a Liberal candidate at Epping in the 1959 General Election. He, too, was defeated.

MOST DEFEATS IN CONSECUTIVE MATCHES

Hampshire endured a run of nine consecutive defeats in 1904. This bleak record was later equalled in 1946.

A FULL SET

Philip Mead is the only Hampshire player to score a century against each of the other first-class counties.

A FULL SET (2)

Gordon Greenidge made a century for Hampshire against all the other counties except Leicestershire. However, he rectified the omission by hitting two hundreds against that county for the West Indies. His last appearance on a Hampshire ground was for the West Indies in 1988. Before a packed Northlands Road, he hit a memorable 103. He therefore registered a hundred against all the 17 counties at the time in all forms of cricket.

NEARLY A FULL SET

Roy Marshall scored a century against every other county except Worcestershire. His highest score against them was 99. Earlier in his career he had struck a career-defining century against Hampshire, hitting 138 for the touring West Indians at Northlands Road in 1950. Durham were not a first-class county during the careers of Marshall or Greenidge.

BATTED ON ALL FOUR DAYS

Liam Dawson's innings of 134 not out against Kent at Tunbridge Wells in 2012 was spread over all four days of the County Championship match. A rain-soaked ground restricted play to 15.1 overs on the first day, which finished with Dawson on five. Only 18.3 overs were bowled on the second day. When play was abandoned in mid-afternoon, one report commented that the ground looked more suited to water polo. Dawson had now progressed to 22. The third day was relatively somewhat better. A further 44.2 overs were possible and Dawson had now passed his century and was 111 not out at close of play. He was still at the crease when Jimmy Adams declared the Hampshire innings on the last morning. After two innings forfeitures, the match was eventually drawn.

CHANGING TEAM

In 1900, no fewer than 41 different men appeared for Hampshire in their 22 matches during the season; 11 of whom played in only one match.

RICHARD GILLIAT

Richard Gilliat virtually severed his ties with the county after he retired from the game in 1978 to take up a career in the City and then at Charterhouse School. He has, therefore, become almost the forgotten man of Hampshire cricket. And yet he was indisputably the most successful of all the county's captains. He was groomed for the job by Desmond Eagar after leaving Cambridge University with Blues in each year from 1964 to 1967. He led Hampshire to the most surprising of all championship titles in 1973. Rain cruelly robbed Hampshire of a second consecutive championship in the following season and, though they played less convincingly, they only just missed out again in 1975, finishing third. No other Hampshire captain can match this sequence in successive seasons. He also captained the side to Sunday League success, Hampshire's first one-day titles, in 1975 and 1978. Gilliat always put his side's needs first, and often sacrificed his wicket in the quest for quick runs. A career average of 30 did not reflect his talent. If he had played for himself more often, he may well have gained a Test cap. A left-handed batsman who originally based his game on defence, he became a free-hitting stroke-maker, whose highest score was 223 not out against Warwickshire at Southampton in 1969. He was also a splendid fielder, first in the gulley and then at mid-off.

HELD GOVERNMENT OFFICE

Three Hampshire cricketers have held Government Office. H.W. Forster (1885–1895) was Junior Lord of the Treasury (1902–1905) and Financial Secretary (War Office 1915–1919). R.E. Prothero (Lord Ernle) (1875–1883) was president of the Board of Agriculture and Fisheries (1915–1919). A.F. Jeffreys (1876–1878) was Parliamentary Secretary Local Government Board in 1915. Forster became president of MCC in 1919. At the end of his term in office he was made Lord Lepe and appointed Governor-General of Australia.

FIRST FIRST-CLASS CENTURY

The county's first first-class century was scored by Charles Frank Lucas against Surrey at The Oval in August 1866. He opened the innings and was last out having made 135 out of 281, hitting six fours.

GORDON GREENIDGE

Body and soul went into every cricket shot played by Gordon Greenidge. He sprang into action to unfurl the most destructive and uninhibited strokes. The frightening factor for bowlers was that it was so calculating. Checked strokes were not in his psyche, though he could play the most delicate of late cuts. Right-handed and compactly built, he drove mightily and cut, pulled and hooked with relish. His technique was orthodox and faultless. Greenidge was never a great improviser. He really had no need to be so, such was his power. He hit the ball stunningly hard. He was extremely quick on his feet, enabling him to play both pace and spin bowling with equal facility. There was also the famous Greenidge limp. Pulled muscles and injured ankles, knees and back were to ring alarm bells in opposition dressing rooms, for the sight of a lame Greenidge was normally a precursor to a century. He even scored a century on one leg and with one hand, against Northamptonshire at Southampton in 1985. He claimed such handicaps made him concentrate harder. Greenidge announced his arrival on the county scene by hitting John Snow for a six out of Dean Park, Bournemouth. The ball took five minutes to find. The event was a foretaste of what was to follow. In the ensuing years he bombarded cars, windows and greenhouses, as well as commentary boxes on Hampshire's ground and many more further afield. He twice hit 13 sixes in an innings. At one stage Greenidge held the record for the highest individual score in all domestic one-day competitions. His range was therefore complete. What he might have achieved in Twenty20 cricket can only be a matter of speculation. Greenidge's injuries deprived cricket of one of its most brilliant all-round fielders. He had started to field in the slips during Hampshire's 1973 championship season, but his speed over the ground, the awesome power of his arm and the accuracy of his throw made him a formidable outfielder. His party piece was to stand over the ball on the boundary daring the batsman to take another run. Greenidge's final appearance at Southampton for the West Indies, in a one-day match against Hampshire in 1988, exemplified his special talent. He took an hour over his first seven runs. Once set, however, he literally picked on each of Hampshire's bowlers in turn, hitting them repeatedly to or over the boundary to reach his century on the stroke of lunch an hour later. It was a masterly and joyous display.

HAMPSHIRE CRICKET

Due to financial difficulties emanating from a deficit from the sale of the club's former headquarters at Northlands Road, and the cost of development of a new ground, The Rose Bowl, at West End, new arrangements to sustain the county's cricket were required. As a result, Hampshire County Cricket Club, which effectively ceased to exist on 19 December 2001, was replaced by Hampshire Cricket, part of Rose Bowl plc. The new enterprise came into being on 1 November 2001 with its business being managed by a board of directors. The new chairman was Rod Bransgrove, who still presides over matters today. It was a new business model for managing cricket in the UK.

HIGHEST INDIVIDUAL FIRST-CLASS INNINGS

316 ..............R.H. Moore v Warwickshire, Bournemouth, 1937
311* ............J.P. Crawley v Nottinghamshire, The Rose Bowl, 2005
304 ..............R.M. Poore v Somerset, Taunton, 1899
301* ............J.P. Crawley v Nottinghamshire, Nottingham, 2004
300* ............M.A. Carberry v Yorkshire, The Rose Bowl, 2011
280* ............C.P. Mead v Nottinghamshire, Southampton, 1921
272 ..............J.P. Crawley v Kent, Canterbury, 2002
268 ..............E.G. Wynyard v Yorkshire, Southampton, 1896
262* ............J.H.K. Adams v Nottinghamshire, Nottingham, 2006
259 ..............C.G. Greenidge v Sussex, Southampton, 1975
258* ............C.B. Fry v Gloucestershire, Southampton, 1911

John Crawley's innings against Kent was on his first-class debut for the county.

HIGHEST INNINGS IN FIRST-CLASS CRICKET

The county's highest individual innings in first-class cricket is 316 by R.H. 'Dick' Moore against Warwickshire at Bournemouth in 1937. Hampshire's captain at the time, he opened the innings and was last out, having hit his runs off 509 balls in 380 minutes, with three sixes and 43 fours. Moore reached his century off the last ball before lunch and progressed to 187 by tea. He reached his double century to take the score to 354 in only 280 minutes. He gave only one chance – when he was on 256. Unfortunately, Dick Moore's innings never quite received the publicity it deserved as Lancashire and England bodyline hero Eddie Paynter hit 322 on the same day along the coast at Hove.

HENRY HORTON

Henry Horton was a great fighter with infinite powers of concentration. He relished the battle, especially when the odds were stacked against him. His sheer doggedness and refusal to accept defeat saved many games for Hampshire, or turned a seemingly lost cause into prosperity. In his book *Test Outcast*, Roy Marshall wrote that if he wanted one man from all those that he had seen to complete his side then it would be Henry Horton. There can be no higher praise. Horton was renowned for his eccentric stance. It was likened to a man sitting on a shooting stick. Silver-haired and invariably capless, he stood low at the crease, with the bat angled at some 45 degrees, and his weight firmly planted on the front foot. From a minimal backlift, he could play all types of bowling off both front and back feet. He was an accumulator of runs, pushing rather than hitting boundaries. His strengths were his front foot driving and his leg side play, though he invariably looked to score in the V. Henry Horton was the classic late developer. Born in Colwell Green, Herefordshire, on 18 April 1923, he played for Worcestershire, with no success at all, from 1946–49. He concentrated on his career as a professional footballer but on his transfer to Southampton in 1951/52, he played a few games of cricket on the County Ground as part of pre-season training. Arthur Holt noted his talent. Horton spent much of the summer of 1952 nursing a knee injury but in August the Hampshire coach asked him to turn out for the Club and Ground team. He scored a couple of centuries, but mindful of his previous experience of county cricket still decided to concentrate on football. At the beginning of the following summer, however, the persuasive Holt inveigled him to sign for Hampshire. Horton made steady progress before, at the age of 36, embarking on the most productive years of his career. In the four years from 1959 he scored 8,904 runs (average 40.84) including 18 centuries. He headed the Hampshire batting averages in 1965 at the age of 42. Horton eventually retired in 1967 when he lost his place to Richard Gilliat. He had played in 405 matches, scoring 21,536 runs (average 33.49) including 32 centuries and holding 254 catches, all after the age of 30. His achievements were quite phenomenal. After his playing days, this lifelong bachelor returned to his roots to become a Worcestershire coach. He also umpired from 1973–76.

COUNTY CHAMPIONS (1)

County Championship table 1961:

	P	W	L	D	ND	Bonus	Pts	Avge
Hampshire	32	19	7	6	–	32	268	8.37
Yorkshire	32	17	5	10	–	34	250	7.81
Middlesex	28	15	6	6	1	26	214	7.64

Hampshire were popular winners of their first County Championship title. The romantics recalled the Hambledon epoch. Some were pleased to see the breaking of the Surrey/Yorkshire monopoly as champion county. Virtually all heralded the spirit of their cricket engendered by their charismatic captain, Colin Ingleby-Mackenzie. The race to the title was a three-horse one all season between the eventual top three counties. Hampshire's start was a faltering one, registering only three wins in their first eight matches by the end of May. When all looked lost as Somerset gained a first innings lead of 102 at Bournemouth, Roy Marshall then set up a marvellous victory with perhaps the best innings of his career. He turned the game around with a commanding knock of 212 in only 260 minutes. Mervyn Burden then administered the coup de grace with 7-72. This win was the first of six consecutive victories that took the county to the top of the table for the first time on 23 June. That lead lasted barely a week. Challengers Middlesex defeated them comprehensively at Lord's to take the lead but by 4 August, after five further successes, Hampshire had returned to the top. Unlike 1959, it was a lead they never lost. The match which clinched the championship at Bournemouth against bogey team Derbyshire, who had halted Hampshire's challenge three years earlier, has long passed into the county's folklore. Derbyshire gained a first innings lead of 12 (318–306), but Hampshire lost two early wickets in wiping off the arrears. However, Marshall batted superbly until close of play on the second day when the county were 113 ahead for the loss of only one more wicket. Marshall (86) was out early next morning to a sinful catch but the charge was taken up resplendently by Peter Sainsbury (73) and Mike Barnard (61), two Hampshire-born players. By virtually playing tip and run, interspersed by the odd boundary, they added 99 runs in 68 minutes. Derbyshire were left to score 252 in 192 minutes. On a wicket more conducive to spin, Derek Shackleton gave a masterclass of seam and cut as he dismissed the first four batsmen for 24. He finished with 6-39 as their opponents were bowled out for 111.

Danny Livingstone earned Hampshire immortality, when at 4.08pm, he took the catch on the midwicket boundary to seal the title. Many have since commented, particularly in Yorkshire, that Hampshire gained the title through a series of generous declarations. It is a myth. In 15 of their 19 games they dismissed the opposition twice – the same as Yorkshire. And

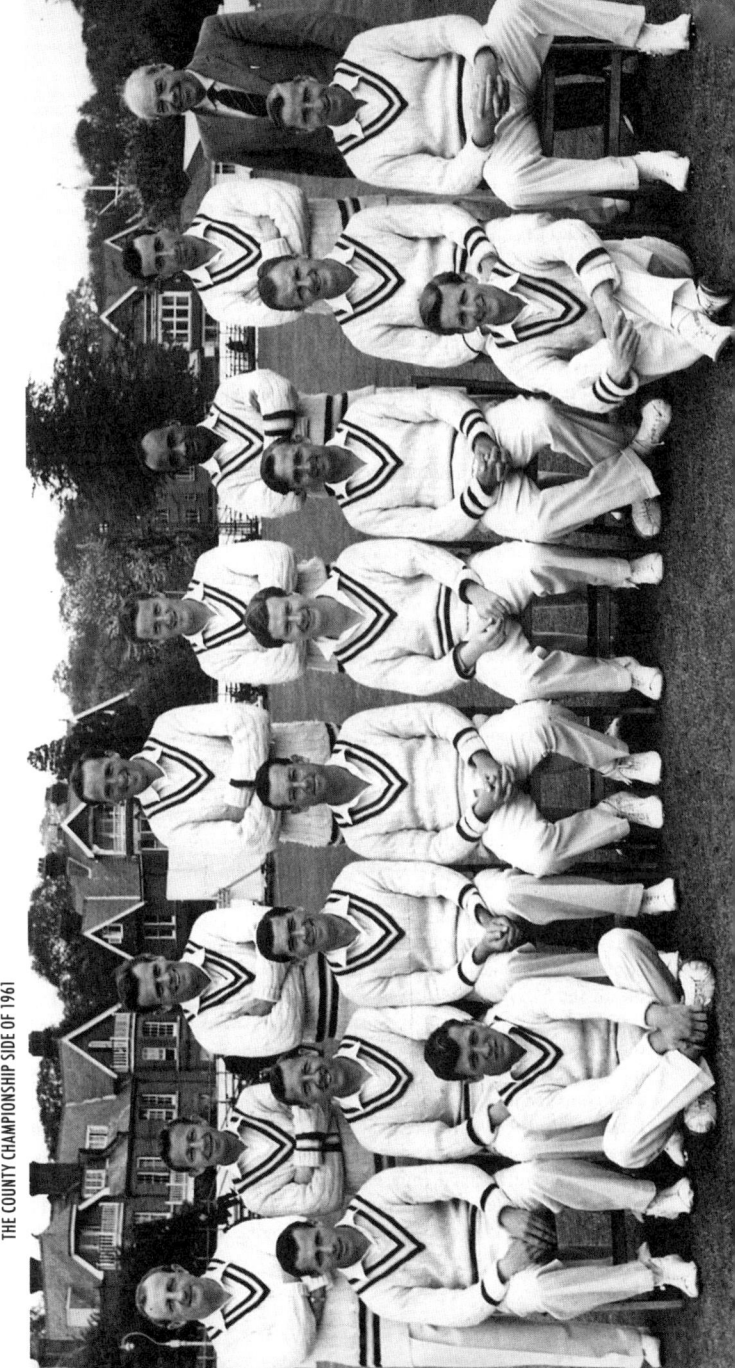

THE COUNTY CHAMPIONSHIP SIDE OF 1961

Hampshire outscored them with the bat. One change in the rules certainly did favour the county. In 1961 there was an experimental rule which prevented captains from enforcing the follow-on. Thus, England captain Peter May, after his Surrey side had lost only six wickets in two innings, eventually set Hampshire 308 in 320 minutes at The Oval. Again, a glorious innings by Marshall (153 in 220 minutes) settled the issue as the county romped home by five wickets with an hour to spare. The match exemplified Hampshire's ability to seize the opportunity when it arose. Another instance was against Gloucestershire at Portsmouth. Rain washed out the second day, after having curtailed play on the first. It therefore seemed a case of playing for first innings bonus points. However, Ingleby-Mackenzie had other ideas. Without consulting his side he declared Hampshire's first innings at 96/0 after 19 overs on the third morning, still 80 runs in arrears. Again, Marshall was in full spate, having made an unbeaten 71 in 70 minutes. The Bajan and his opening partner, Jimmy Gray, were furious. However, their opponents then struggled against the unrelenting accuracy of Derek Shackleton (4-27 in 19 overs). Gloucestershire's captain, Arthur Milton, then declared with eight wickets down leaving Hampshire a target of 199 in 137 minutes – a rate of 88 an hour, a tall order in those days. The champions-elect went for the runs all down the order and thanks to some rumbustious blows by fast bowler David 'Butch' White, they triumphed with two minutes to spare. The final declaration success was against Essex at Cowes on the Isle of Wight. Matches between the two counties were generally dull affairs but mindful that the wicket was deteriorating rapidly and that Marshall was injured, Trevor Bailey must have felt that the odds were stacked in his favour when he declared with 215 minutes remaining and Hampshire 240 in arrears. It looked like game, set and match as the home side slid to 35/4. However, Ingleby-Mackenzie then played the innings of his life. Despite his brilliance, 72 runs were still required with 69 minutes and only four wickets remaining. Enter Marshall, hobbling badly, with a runner.

He scored 36 and his with effervescent captain knocked off the remaining runs in only 44 minutes. Ingleby-Mackenzie ended on a career best 132 not out. Five of the side, Jimmy Gray, Peter Sainsbury, Mike Barnard, Malcolm Heath and Mervyn Burden, were county-born. In their formative years they came under the guidance of the much cherished Arthur Holt, who developed the famed Holt's Colts. Hampshire came into the season with virtually all the side at the peak of their powers. Marshall and Henry Horton both passed 2,000 runs and Jimmy Gray scored 1,950. Sainsbury, Ingleby-Mackenzie and Livingstone also scored more than 1,000. Dennis Baldry batted usefully at the start of the season, particularly in a draw against Yorkshire at Headingley. His replacement, Barnard, came into the side at the latter part of the summer, and turned the tide in Hampshire's favour with an exceptional century (114 not out) against Warwickshire at Southampton. All the batsmen, except

Gray and Baldry, recorded their highest championship scores to date during the season. With the ball, the evergreen Derek Shackleton was omnipotent, taking 158 wickets, the best return in the country in the competition. Butch White, newcomer Alan Wassell, Sainsbury and Malcolm Heath all took over 50 wickets. Mervyn Burden took 22 in the two wins over Somerset, and 45 in all. His 8-38 at Frome was the season's best figures by any bowler in the championship. Jimmy Gray chipped in with 31 wickets. The catching was reliable, as was Leo Harrison's wicketkeeping. Having made his debut in 1939, it was the crowning glory of his career. It was a wonderful all-round team effort. Only 15 men played in the championship side all season.

MOST RUNS IN INDIA

Hampshire's John Glennie Greig holds the record for the most number of runs scored by an England-qualified player in Indian domestic cricket. The short, Indian-born right-handed batsman played 42 matches in the country between 1893/94 and 1920/21, scoring 2,801 runs (average 43.09), including five centuries. He was often known as the 'Indian W.G. Grace'. Greig appeared with distinction in 77 matches for Hampshire between 1901 and 1922, hitting ten centuries including 249 not out against Lancashire at Liverpool in the first of those years. He was an army officer, who later became a Roman Catholic priest, ordained in Rome. He was Hampshire secretary from 1921–30, and died at Milford-on-Sea in 1958.

THE INDIANS

Between 1932 and 2002 Hampshire played the touring Indian sides 14 times, winning twice and losing on five occasions. Seven matches were drawn. The two victories were in the first encounter in 1932 (by an innings and 103 runs) and in 1990 (by seven wickets).

KEVAN JAMES – WORLD RECORD HOLDER

Hampshire's matches against the Indians produced much good cricket, but no occurrence was as dramatic as that on the first day of the fixture in 1996. Kevan James interrupted India's serene start to their innings by dismissing four batsmen in four balls. His victims were two of the greatest batsmen ever to grace a cricket field in Sachin Tendulkar (caught at short leg) and Rahul Dravid (lbw), as well as Vikram Vathore and Sanjay Manjrekar. The unsung left-handed all-rounder had earlier taken the wicket of Ajay Jadeja. They were the only wickets to fall in the day and James finished the innings with 5-74. However, he still wasn't done. On the following day (Sunday), James then struck a commanding 103, while nursing a hangover from his overnight celebrations. He is unique in being the only man ever to take four wickets in four balls and score a century in the same match.

THE PARSIS

The first Indian visitors to England were the Parsis sides of 1886 and 1888. They played a total of five matches in the county on those tours, though not against Hampshire.

TIGHT FINISHES

Matches between Hampshire and India produced several tight finishes. In 1936, the tourists won by two runs. In 1952, India were set 106 runs to win in 55 minutes but they finished on 100/8. In 1959, the tourists ended on 96/8, chasing 171 in 108 minutes for victory. On their next visit in 1967, it was Hampshire who achieved an honourable draw. Set 293 in 217 minutes, the county closed on 286/9. Finally, in 1971, India eased home by five wickets with ten minutes to spare.

TOURED INDIA

The following Hampshire players appeared in first-class cricket in India while on MCC/England tours: Stuart Boyes and George Brown (1926/27), Derek Shackleton (1951/52), Butch White (1961/62), Robin Smith (1992/93), Kevin Pietersen (2005/06 and 2008/09 as captain), and Shaun Udal (2005/06). Michael Carberry toured with the England Lions in 2007/08. The tour made by Boyes and Brown was in pre-partition India and the team therefore played at venues now in Pakistan. Arthur Hill and Colin Heseltine also played in Lord Hawke's Team to India (and Ceylon, now Sri Lanka) in 1892/93. Lord Tennyson took his own team to India in 1937/38. It included his Hampshire colleagues Neil McCorkell and Tommy Jameson. Alec Hosie also played for and against Tennyson's team.

LONGEST GAP BETWEEN APPEARANCES

The following players experienced a gap of ten years or more between appearances for Hampshire in first-class cricket:

Arthur Richards	19 years 15 days	(1884–1903)
Harry Baldwin	18 years 4 days	(1877–1895)
Alastair MacLeod	14 years 305 days	(1920–1935)
James Darby	12 years 358 days	(1884–1897)
Alan Mullally	12 years 27 days	(1988–2000)
E.G. Wynyard	11 years 196 days	(1883–1895)
Henry Bethune	11 years 287 days	(1885–1897)
John Manners	10 years 336 days	(1936–1947)

SMOKE STOPPED PLAY

In Hampshire's match against Leicestershire at Aylestone Road in 1939, play was held up for seven minutes on the second day due to smoke from a bonfire in a nearby garden.

TAKEN ILL AND DIED

Tragically, after scoring 40 and 39 against Lancashire at Southampton in the first match of the 1897 season, H.F. Ward was taken ill with sunstroke during the game and died in hospital of typhoid fever a few days later. He was 24 years old.

COLIN INGLEBY-MACKENZIE

Colin Ingleby-Mackenzie was a very special man, a complete one-off. He was one of those rare people who seemed to breeze through life as if they did not have a care in the world. He possessed an engaging charismatic personality and immense charm in spades. Life was for living to the full. He was a captain who was never afraid to risk losing in pursuit of victory. Possessor of the instincts of a born gambler, he was a master of keeping the opposition interested in a run-chase, while maximising his own team's chance of winning the match. Ingleby-Mackenzie's intrinsic warm-heartedness, integrity and persuasive powers were valuable assets in negotiating declarations with opposing captains. There were very few who were not persuaded to make a game of it in the interests of their side and above all spectators. Counties liked games against Hampshire in his era as they played cricket in the right spirit, allied to which he was one of the most loved men on the county circuit. He never lost sight of the fact that although winning was the prime objective, cricket was also a game to be enjoyed. Some of his philosophical statements have passed into cricket legend. Ingleby-Mackenzie's assertions that the team's success is founded on 'wine, women and song' and that one of his few disciplinary rules is that his team 'be in bed by breakfast' have stood the test of time. There was also the occasion when, while on an overseas tour, the manager was concerned about his team's nocturnal conviviality. He suggested on the eve of one important match that the players ought to be in bed by 11pm. His irrepressible captain responded with the quip 'that the match starts at 11.30'. Umpires also became used to requests to put his transistor radio in their pocket so that he could learn the racing results during the afternoon's play. Ingleby-Mackenzie was a natural to lead ambassadorial teams abroad. He captained teams to all parts of the globe, making friends and enhancing the game's interest and image in the process. It was predestined that he would one day become a highly influential president of MCC. His networking skills and force of personality were to culminate in women being able to become

MCC members and gain access to the hallowed pavilion at Lord's. This achievement and Hampshire's winning of their first County Championship in 1961 is his enduring legacy.

NO SINGING

When Hampshire were presented with their championship pennant at Buckingham Palace at the end of the 1961 season, Butch White is alleged to have been asked whether Hampshire would continue with their 'wine, women and song' philosophy in the following year. He reputedly replied that they may do without the song!

THE SINGING BOWLERS

Ernest Remnant, a slow left-arm bowler who played for the county between 1908 and 1922, used to sing quietly but audibly as he bowled. His refrain during his run-up was 'dah dah dah' followed by 'take that' as he bowled. Derek Shackleton was sometimes heard to break into a ditty which began, 'I'll slap thee on the belly with a big flat fish.'

LATE ARRIVALS

Several Hampshire players arrived late at Canterbury for their match against Kent in 1921. After winning the toss, Hampshire had no option but to bat until the players arrived. They would have preferred to field first as the wicket was drying out after rain and favoured the bowlers. Hampshire were duly shot out for 68, all the wickets being taken by spin bowlers, Frank Woolley and 'Tich' Freeman. In the second innings, the future Hampshire president Harry Altham played the knock of his life, scoring 141 in 210 minutes. However, it was not enough to prevent a Kent victory by eight wickets.

LONGEST-LIVED PLAYERS

The longest-lived of all Hampshire cricketers was Edward Apsey English. Born in Dorking, Surrey, on 1 January 1864, he played 18 matches for Hampshire between 1898 and 1901. A middle-order right-handed batsman, his highest score was 98 against the county of his birth in 1898. He was caught off the last ball of the match as he attempted to reach a much coveted century. He was 102 years and 248 days old when he died at Tiverton, Devon, on 5 September 1966. In February 2013, former wicketkeeper Neil McCorkell died in Johannesburg three weeks shy of his 101st birthday. At the time of writing, three Hampshire players are into their 90s: John Manners (born 1914), Vic Cannings (1919) and Leo Harrison (1922).

ISLE OF WIGHT CRICKETERS

Isle of Wight-born cricketers are a new, and increasingly influential, factor on the county cricket scene, both in Hampshire and elsewhere. In recent years, slow left-arm bowler Danny Briggs and right-arm fast-medium David Griffiths have given a high profile to cricket on the island because of their performances for Hampshire. Before their arrival, only seven Isle of Wight cricketers had played for the county. The last was in 1927, though Mark Garaway who played three matches for Hampshire between 1996 and 1999, deserves mention. He was born in Swindon, but was educated on the island and played his club cricket for Ventnor. However, none matched the profile of the two contemporary players. Griffiths (debut 2006) played 36 times for the county, taking 105 wickets. He moved to Kent at the end of last season. Briggs (debut 2009) has claimed 110 wickets in 44 appearances and has played for England in ODIs and Twenty20s.

NEWPORT, ISLE OF WIGHT

Hampshire played two matches at Newport Recreation Ground on the Isle of Wight in 1938 and 1939. In the first, the county defeated Northamptonshire by seven wickets. Stuart Boyes enjoyed a fine all-round match. He scored a career best 104 (including 13 fours) in 110 minutes in Hampshire's first innings before spinning out six batsmen for 40 in the opponents' second knock. Hampshire won the match on a Neil McCorkell six, with only five minutes remaining. In the following year the boot was on the other foot as Middlesex crushed the county by an innings and 25 runs.

COWES, ISLE OF WIGHT

Hampshire returned to the Isle of Wight to play at J. Samuel White's ground at West Cowes between 1956 and 1962. They played one match in each year, winning three, drawing three and losing one. Colin Ingleby-Mackenzie enjoyed the venue immensely scoring an unbeaten 130 against Worcestershire in 1956 and a career best 132 not out versus Essex in Hampshire's championship year of 1961. Roy Marshall (107) and Henry Horton (114 not out) both hit centuries to set up victory against Nottinghamshire in 1957. Derek Shackleton also took 7-81 in that match. He went on to take five wickets in an innings on three further occasions at the ground.

ALEX JOHNSTON

Contemporary pundits alleged that Alex Johnston was the best of all Hampshire's soldier batsmen. He took a sabbatical between leaving Sandhurst and joining his regiment by working as a cowboy for a year in the USA. Service duties impinged on his appearances in county cricket. His most impressive season was in 1912. In a dismally wet summer with unpredictable pitches, he scored 1,044 runs (average 54.94), with a century in each innings, 175 (his highest score) and 100 not out, against Warwickshire at Coventry. He also made the top score of 89 in the Gentlemen's first innings against the Players at Lord's. A contemporary said the innings, played against the S.F. Barnes XI on a wicket loaded in the bowlers' favour, was one of the best he ever saw. Johnston served with distinction in the First World War. He was wounded four times, mentioned in despatches on five occasions and was awarded the Military Cross. Given that he was a member of the original Expeditionary Force, and was in France for three years, he was lucky to have escaped with his life. He ended the war with the rank of Brigadier General. His wounds left him with one leg four inches shorter than the other. Johnston could only bat with a runner when cricket resumed in peace-time. However, he was effectively banned from appearing in first-class cricket because of his disability. He played football, hockey and polo at regimental level. He appeared in 108 matches for Hampshire between 1902 and 1920, scoring 5,442 runs (average 30.74), including ten centuries.

MEDAL FOR SAVING A LIFE

E.G. Wynyard was awarded a Royal Humane Society medal for saving the life of a Swiss peasant on Lake Davos in December 1893. The citation referred to the fact that he put himself 'at great personal risk'.

ALEC KENNEDY

No day was too long for Alec Kennedy. Cricket has had few, if any, more conscientious triers. He could, and did, keep going for hours on end. Despite a chassé en route, his run-up was so automated that after a while, 'stepping stones' would appear on the surface indicating where he had mechanically placed his feet. Batsmen were required to combat the same metronome efficiently when he delivered the ball. Kennedy would simply wear away a spot on a good length and bowl, at medium pace, with subtle changes in the speed of delivery, his stock in-swing ball, and with the classic variation of the leg-cutter on a good wicket, he would wait for the batsman to self-destruct. On any pitch influenced by the weather, he was often unplayable. Only six men in the history of cricket have taken more than his 2,874 wickets. Alexander Stuart Kennedy was born in Edinburgh on 24 January 1891. His parents moved to Southampton while he was a child. On leaving school at the age of 14 he joined the Hampshire staff. He took 100 wickets in a season on 15 occasions and performed the double of 100 wickets and 1,000 runs five times. He took three hat-tricks. Kennedy's best season was in 1922 when he took 205 wickets, a haul which earned him selection for the MCC tour to South Africa the following winter. He was England's outstanding bowler with 31 wickets (average 19.32) in the Test series, yet never represented his country again. There were once (unfair) doubts about his action and perhaps this factor mitigated against further test consideration. Kennedy had a final fine all-round game against Warwickshire at Portsmouth in 1923, when he compiled his highest score, 163 not out, and took nine wickets in the match for 77 runs. RC Robertson-Glasgow commented, 'His batting varied from the studious to the violent … (he) knew all the bowlers as well as they knew themselves.' There are no humorous stories about Alec Kennedy. However, Robertson-Glasgow wrote, 'As an adviser on bowling, I never found his equal, and in a swift, soft flow of words, he would sweep away doubt and resolve mysteries.' He brought these gifts to bear upon his retirement at the age of 45 in 1936. He coached at Cheltenham College and then in Johannesburg from 1947 to 1954. He returned to Southampton, where he ran a tobacconist and stationers shop near The Bargate. He died at Hythe on 15 November 1959.

ALEC KENNEDY MISCELLANY

Alec Kennedy's career total of 2,874 wickets has been exceeded by only six other bowlers.

Between 1920 and 1923, he captured 698 wickets for Hampshire during the county cricket seasons. In all matches during this period, including the MCC tour to South Africa in 1922/23, he harvested 805 wickets.

He took 233 wickets in the 1922 calendar year, a record for any Hampshire player. This total included 205 in the English season, also the most by a Hampshire bowler.

Kennedy headed the Hampshire bowling averages on 11 occasions between 1912 and 1935.

He returned figures of 8-11 against Glamorgan at Cardiff Arms Park in 1921. He claimed all of those wickets before lunch.

SECOND-CLASS COUNTIES COMPETITION

Between 1888 and 1893 Hampshire played in a second-class counties competition. Their opponents were Cheshire, Derbyshire, Essex, Hertfordshire, Leicestershire, Norfolk, Northamptonshire, Somerset, Staffordshire and Warwickshire. Over the six-year period, Hampshire played 36 matches, winning nine, losing 20 and drawing seven.

MINOR COUNTIES CHAMPIONSHIP

Hampshire ran a second XI in the Minor Counties Championship from 1949 to 1952 inclusive. In these four seasons they finished third, 11th, 16th and 24th respectively out of 27. Five future members of the County Championship-winning side of 1961 – Peter Sainsbury, Malcolm Heath, Mike Barnard, Mervyn Burden and Colin Ingleby-Mackenzie – made their first competitive outing in the county's colours in these matches. Arthur Holt, Hampshire's coach, led by example in making the highest score in these games when he struck 185 against Kent second XI at Broadstairs in 1952.

HIGHEST SCORE ON FIRST-CLASS DEBUT

No Hampshire player has ever scored a century on his first-class debut when appearing for the county. The closest to achieving the feat was Paul Whitaker who reached 94 against Leicestershire at Grace Road, Leicester, in 1994.

C.B. LLEWELLYN

Charles Bennett 'Buck' Llewellyn is Hampshire's man of 'firsts'. He was the county's first overseas registration, the first Hampshire player to complete the 'double', the first and so far, only, Hampshire batsman whose maiden first-class century has been a double hundred, and the first Hampshire player to score 100 runs and take ten wickets in the same match. Most importantly, however, in a historical context, he was the first black cricketer to play Test cricket for South Africa, though it was not acknowledged at the time. He was born in Pietermaritzburg on 29 September 1876 to a Welsh father and a mother who came from St. Helena. He made his first-class debut for Natal in March 1895 and made his first Test appearance in the following season. In 1899 he decided, upon the recommendation of R.M. Poore, to qualify for Hampshire. In that year, he made 72 and took 8-132 on his debut against the Australians, a record analysis on debut for Hampshire. His feats in his first full year of 1901 were sensational. He completed the 'double' in all matches. His 121 wickets for Hampshire included a career best 8-71 at Leicester. Against the touring South Africans he scored 216 in three hours, which was to remain the highest score of his career. In 1902 Llewellyn headed both the Hampshire batting and bowling averages and such was his stature that though having previously played for South Africa, he was one of 14 players chosen for England's side against Australia at Edgbaston. In the following winter he went back to South Africa where he took 25 wickets in three Tests against the Australians on their way home. His tally still remains a record for South Africa in a three-Test series. After such a startling entry into full-time cricket, and non-stop travelling, Llewellyn suffered a reaction. In a weak bowling side he was often over-worked and unless Hesketh Pritchard was available, rarely received any worthwhile support. Consequently, his bowling lost much of its penetration and he had to await the blossoming of Jack Newman in 1908 to regain his form. He enjoyed a splendid final season in 1910, when he and Newman took 289 of the 422 wickets that fell to Hampshire bowlers. He again performed the 'double' and was named as one of *Wisden*'s Five Cricketers of the Year. Following a disagreement over terms, he then left Hampshire at the end of the season and took up a more lucrative engagement with Accrington in the Lancashire League.

Apart from appearances for South Africa in Australia and the Triangular Tournament in England in 1912, it marked the end of his first-class career. Llewellyn was hugely prolific, especially with the ball, in the leagues and continued to play the game until he was 62 years of age. He died in Chertsey in Surrey, aged 87.

TIGER STOPPED PLAY

An unusual incident held up play in a Southern League match between the Hampshire Academy and South Wilts at the Ageas Bowl in May 2011. A member of the public raised concern that there was a white tiger hiding in a field close to the ground. Police officers were sent to investigate along with a helicopter and thermal imaging cameras. When no body heat was detected police moved in and found it was a cuddly toy tiger. However, so large and life-like was the toy that contingency plans had been put in place to close the adjacent M27. Help was also sought from animal experts at nearby Marwell Zoo, who offered advice and were prepared to send a team armed with tranquilliser darts. Golfers at the ground were also told to go indoors. Play in the match resumed after a 20-minute break.

AVERAGE POSITION IN THE COUNTY CHAMPIONSHIP

Since Hampshire's admission to the County Championship in 1895, their average position in the table has been ninth. Their average position in each decade since the above date has been as follows:

	Average position	Best	Worst
1895–1899	9.8	8	12
1900–1909	11.9	7	16 (last)
1910–1919	7.5	5	11
1920–1929	9.4	6	13
1930–1939	13.0	8	16
1946–1949	12.7	9	16
1950–1959	9.3	2	14
1960–1969	9.0	1	12
1970–1979	7.7	1	12
1980–1989	6.9	2	17
1990–1999	10.7	3	15
2000–2009	7.2	2	16

MALCOLM MARSHALL – A SUPERHERO

It can be seen from the previous entry that Hampshire's best decade was in the 1980s. On the basis that 'bowlers win matches' the determining factor for their success in that period was Malcolm Marshall. Marshall toured England with the West Indies in 1980, 1984 and 1988. In the years in which he played for Hampshire in that decade, their average position was 5.3. Hampshire never finished lower than seventh and were second once and third twice. For good measure, Hampshire were also third in 1990. In these eight seasons in which he played full-time for the county between 1981 and 1990, he took 685 wickets at the extraordinarily low average of 17.28 runs per wicket on covered wickets.

MOST CHAMPIONSHIP MATCHES
PLAYED IN A SEASON

In the seasons 1960, 1961 and 1962, Hampshire played 32 matches in the County Championship in each of those summers, a record for the county.

STRANGE GOINGS-ON (1)

There were strange goings-on on the final day of Hampshire's match with Glamorgan at Bournemouth in 1969. Hampshire led by 95 runs with nine wickets in hand when rain stopped play at 1pm. It rained all afternoon and tea was taken at 3.45pm. After a conference between the two captains, Roy Marshall and Tony Lewis, and the umpires, both captains believed the match had been abandoned. Both sides changed, Marshall and Lewis shook hands and it was still raining when the Hampshire team left the ground at 4.30pm. Not long after their departure the rain eased and the umpires, Peter Wight and Lloyd Budd, a former Hampshire player, decided play was possible. The Glamorgan side changed hurriedly back into their whites, some of them even putting their flannels over their civvies, and took the field. The umpires waited the obligatory two minutes for the Hampshire batsmen to reach the middle. When nobody arrived they called play and then awarded the match to Glamorgan. Hampshire appealed the decision. Both captains, the umpires and Hampshire secretary Desmond Eagar then attended a committee meeting at Lord's in July. It was agreed that there had been a genuine misunderstanding that the match had been called off and the result was amended to a draw.

ROY MARSHALL

Roy Marshall was a man apart. His vivid stroke play will forever live in the memory of those who flocked to county grounds between 1955 and 1972 just to see him bat. He was one of those whose dismissal almost embarrassed the other players on the field. The crowd would sigh, adjourn to the beer tent or pavilion bar, fidget for the rest of the day or just leave the ground. Many would attempt to establish if he was batting before making their way to the ground in the first instance. For one who built his innings on a knife-edge, his run aggregate (30,303), tally of centuries (60) and average (36.03) were remarkable. He once hit the first ball of an innings for six. He was the first to play with any regularity the upper-cut for six over third man. Marshall was one of the unluckiest of cricketers. He immediately preceded that era when cricketers were able to ply their talents with impunity all over the world. In the early 1950s, when he first joined Hampshire, he had to serve a three-year qualification period. He was also effectively banned from playing Test cricket for both the West Indies and England. That he was never able to add to his four West Indian Test caps was almost criminal. The only weakness of Frank Worrell's great and charismatic West Indian team of the early 1960s was a reliable opening partner for Conrad Hunte. Marshall, then at the peak of his powers, would surely have filled that role. As it was, he had to content himself with a couple of appearances for a representative West Indian XI at the end of the 1964 English season. Marshall can now be seen as a pivotal figure in Hampshire's history. Before his arrival, Hampshire's batting was a solid, workmanlike affair. He completely transformed that outlook single-handedly as he took the attack to the bowlers. Runs suddenly became easier for his colleagues. He created the image that lasts to this day, of

Hampshire being an attractive batting side. Marshall was the spiritual father of the magnificent stroke-players who have graced Hampshire in the past 35 years. In his final season of 1972, at the age of 42, he scored 203 not out at Derby. By now, the carefree dasher had been replaced by the mature master. His defensive technique was massive, awesome; his shot selection was flawless. The only way he would be dismissed was to get himself out. And that, on reflection, was how it always happened.

COUNTY CHAMPIONS (2)

County Championship table 1973:

	P	W	L	D	Bt	Bw	Pts
Hampshire	20	10	0	10	84	81	265
Surrey	20	9	3	8	71	73	234
Northamptonshire	20	8	4	8	53	75	208

Hampshire's second championship title was one of the most unexpected in the competition's history. They had finished ninth in 1972, a season which also marked the retirement of Roy Marshall. Bowlers Butch White, Bob Cottam, Alan Castell and John Holder had left a year earlier. The bowling resources looked very thin. The bookies' odds of the county winning the championship were 66-1. And yet Hampshire romped home, remaining undefeated, and won more matches than any other county. In nine of their ten victories, they bowled out the opposition twice. In the other win, 19 wickets were taken. Against all expectations it was the bowlers who provided the foundation of their success. They earned more bonus points than any other team in the country, and the 321 wickets were taken at an average cost of only 22 runs each. Three men, Mike Taylor (63), who transferred from Nottinghamshire in the preceding winter, Bob Herman (63) and Tom Mottram (57), effectively enjoying a sabbatical from a career in architecture, took more than 50 wickets. The two left-arm spinners, veteran Peter Sainsbury and the New Zealander David O'Sullivan, weighed in with 49 and 47 respectively. Trevor Jesty claimed 35, three times returning career best figures. O'Sullivan took 37 of his wickets in six matches in the Championship run-in during August. Taylor took 7-53 when the county clinched the championship against Gloucestershire at Bournemouth. The bowlers were supported splendidly by the slip catching of Barry Richards (35 catches) and Gordon Greenidge (36). Wicketkeeper Bob Stephenson claimed 65 dismissals. Captain Richard Gilliat was impassable at mid-off where he held 23 catches. The bedrock of the batting was provided by Richards (1,326 runs at 51) and Greenidge (1,656 runs at 48.70). The pair recorded six century opening partnerships during the season. Gilliat scored two fine centuries during Portsmouth week. The county were in serious danger of defeat on only one occasion, against Gloucestershire at Bristol. Otherwise,

HARRY BALDWIN

apart from a first innings slip against Somerset at Taunton, when they were rescued by Sainsbury's first century (120 not out) since 1964, Hampshire were in the ascendancy. They first led the table after defeating Warwickshire at Coventry by seven wickets on 8 June but a run of draws pulled them down to third place, behind Northamptonshire and Essex on 20 July.

They regained the lead after overwhelming Lancashire by an innings at Southport a week later and were never threatened thereafter. Four of their wins – at Headingley, Coventry, Southport and Worcester – were achieved on perfect batting wickets. The key match was played out in glorious sunshine against Northamptonshire at Southampton in mid-August. The sides were first and second in the table. After losing the toss Hampshire dominated a low-scoring affair. They dismissed their opponents for 108. The wickets were shared, with the unathletic Tom Mottram, setting the tone by brilliantly catching Roy Virgin off his own bowling low to his right. Richards and Greenidge took the reply to 76, and were just starting to open up before Bishen Bedi (6-69) rudely interrupted their progress by luring both batsmen down the track to be stumped. Former Hampshire favourite Bob Cottam (3-49) also reined in the innings so that the lead was restricted to just 59. Mottram (4-27), O'Sullivan (4-50) and Taylor (2-21 in 15 miserly overs) then bowled out Northants for 148, leaving Hampshire 90 to win. An unforgettable duel then ensued between Richards and Bedi. The South African emerged unscathed on 37, to carry his side to a seven-wicket victory just before the end of the second day. Richards regarded his innings as his best of the season. O'Sullivan (11-41 in the match) inspired an overwhelming 295-run win against Nottinghamshire, who were dismissed for only 45 in their second innings, at Bournemouth in the following match. The championship was secured when Hampshire gained their fifth batting point against Gloucestershire two days later, again at Bournemouth. Only 13 players appeared for the county in championship matches. The others not previously mentioned above were David Turner, Richard Lewis and Andy Murtagh.

ELECTED TO THE HOUSE OF COMMONS

Ten Hampshire players have been elected to the House of Commons: F. Compton (South Hants 1880–85; New Forest 1885–92), W. Deedes (East Kent 1857–62), H.W. Forster (Bromley 1892–1919), G.G. Greenwood (Peterborough 1906–18), Sir F.T.A. Hervey-Bathurst (South Wilts 1861–65), A.F. Jeffreys (North Hants 1887–1906), H.C. Lowther (Westmorland 1812–67), J. Mills (Rochester 1831–34), T.A. Smith (Andover 1821–31; Caernarvonshire 1832–37), W. Ward (City of London 1826–31). All were Conservatives except for Greenwood, who was a Liberal.

MOST FIRST-CLASS RUNS FOR HAMPSHIRE

The most number of runs by current players are 8,974 by Jimmy Adams and 7,372 by Michael Carberry.

MOST RUNS IN A SEASON

Given the reduction in the championship programme, it seems almost inconceivable that any man will score 2,000 runs in a season in the future. The feat was performed by nine players: Phil Mead (ten occasions), Roy Marshall (four), Jimmy Gray and Henry Horton (three each), and John Arnold, Gordon Greenidge, Barry Richards, Neville Rogers and Chris Smith (once each). The highest aggregate is Phil Mead's 2,854 in 1928. Gordon Greenidge was the last man to reach the landmark in 1986 (2,035 runs). The most number of runs by a batsman since the introduction of the four-day County Championship in 1993 is 1,737 by John Crawley in 2006.

MOST RUNS FOR HAMPSHIRE
IN FIRST-CLASS CRICKET

1:	48,892	C.P. Mead	14:	15,833	N.T. McCorkell
2:	30,303	R.E. Marshall	15:	15,607	B.A. Richards
3:	22,962	G. Brown	16:	15,292	N.H. Rogers
4:	22,450	J.R. Gray	17:	15,287	C.L. Smith
5:	21,596	J. Arnold	18:	14,925	A.S. Kennedy
6:	21,536	H. Horton	19:	14,753	T.E. Jesty
7:	19,840	C.G. Greenidge	20:	13,904	J.A. Newman
8:	19,576	P.J. Sainsbury	21:	12,660	D.A. Livingstone
9:	18,984	R.A. Smith	22:	12,626	Lord Tennyson
10:	18,683	D.R. Turner	23:	12,212	E.M. Sprot
11:	18,466	H.A.W. Bowell	24:	11,140	A.C.D. Ingleby-
12:	17,401	M.C.J. Nicholas			Mackenzie
13:	16,134	V.P. Terry	25:	10,091	E.D.R. Eagar

PHILIP MEAD

In a Hampshire career from 1905–1936, Charles Philip Mead scored more runs for Hampshire than any other batsman has scored for their county. In doing so he created his own miscellany (see below). That great cricket writer R.C. Robertson-Glasgow (also known as Crusoe) probably captured the essence of Mead's cricket in his book *Cricket Prints*. He wrote, 'He was number four, perhaps two wickets had fallen cheaply; and there the cheapness would end. He emerged from the pavilion with a strong rolling gait; like a longshoreman with a purpose. He pervaded a cricket pitch. He occupied it and encamped on it. He erected a tent with a system of infallible pegging, then posted inexorable centuries. He took guard with the air of a guest who, having been offered a weekend by his host, obstinately decides to reside for six months. Having settled his whereabouts with the umpire, he wiggled the toe of his left boot for some 15 seconds inside the crease, pulled the peak of a cap which seemed all peak, wriggled again, pulled again, then gave a comprehensive stare around him, as if to satisfy himself that no fielder, aware of the task ahead, had brought out a stick of dynamite. Then he leaned forward and looked at you down the pitch quite still, his back looked almost laughably broad.'

A MEAD MISCELLANY

Phil Mead scored 46,268 runs in the County Championship, more than any other player. His tally of 132 championship centuries is also unsurpassed, as is his seasonal aggregate of 2,843 runs in county championship matches in 1928.

Phil Mead has scored the most runs (48,892), most centuries (138) and most double centuries (11) for Hampshire.

Mead twice achieved the rare feat of scoring 1,000 runs in a month. In June 1921, he made 1,159 runs (avge. 96.58). Two years later, he averaged a scarcely credible 152.85 while hitting 1,070 runs in July.

Mead twice scored 3,000 runs in a season in all first-class cricket. He amassed 3,179 (average 69.10) in his great year of 1921 and 3,027 (average 75.67) in 1928.

Mead scored 1,000 runs in 27 consecutive seasons from 1906–36. Only Kent's Frank Woolley has exceeded this figure (28). Woolley was the man who frequently kept Mead out of the England team. He also scored 2,000 runs in a season for Hampshire on ten occasions.

Mead took 892 innings to record 100 centuries in first-class cricket. He achieved the feat at the age of 40 years and 132 days.

Hampshire's reliance on Mead's dependability is demonstrated by the fact that, with two exceptions, he topped their averages every season between 1913 and 1936. John Arnold interrupted the sequence in 1930 and 1932. Only on two occasions between 1913 and 1929 did his seasonal average – on uncovered wickets – fall below 50. On six occasions (1914, 1921, 1922, 1923, 1928 and 1933) he made over 1,000 runs more in the season than his next county colleague, and in 1921 and 1928 he scored more than double the runs of the next man. The feat in 1921 is even more remarkable in that he missed matches due to Test selection.

MORE MEAD

In the period from 1 January 1928 to 31 December 1928, Phil Mead scored 3,745 runs (average 74.90), the highest aggregate by any Hampshire player in a calendar year. He also scored 16 centuries in this period, another record. He celebrated his 41st birthday during this astonishing sequence.

FATHERS AND SONS

The following sets of fathers and sons have played for Hampshire:

Father	Son
E. Barrett	E.I.M. Barrett
C.B. Fry	S. Fry
Sir F.H.H. Bathurst	F.T.A.H. Bathurst and L.H. Bathurst
S. Fry	C.A. Fry
C.R. Gunner	J.H. Gunner
H.A.W. Bowell	N.H. Bowell
O.W. Herman	R.S. Herman
S. Brutton	C.P. Brutton
A.J.L. Hill	A.E.L. Hill
E.L. Ede	E.M.C. Ede
V.P. Terry	S.P. Terry
A.H. Evans	A.J. Evans and R. du B. Evans
T.M. Tremlett	C.T. Tremlett

MOST INNINGS IN A SEASON

Danny Livingstone made 61 visits to the crease in 1961, the most number of innings by a Hampshire player.

MOST NUMBER OF CENTURIES IN A SEASON

The most number of centuries scored in a season by Hampshire batsmen is 25 in 1926 and 1990. Ten different batsmen achieved the landmark in the first of those years, which remains a record for the county.

NEW ZEALAND OVERSEAS PLAYERS

Three New Zealanders have appeared for Hampshire in first-class cricket: David O'Sullivan (1971–73), Craig McMillan (2005) and Shane Bond (2008).

THE NEW ZEALANDERS

Between 1931 and 1999, Hampshire played the New Zealanders nine times. The Kiwis won two matches and seven were drawn. Hampshire also played New Zealand A at Portsmouth in 2000. The visitors maintained their unbeaten record in the county, winning by two wickets. A number of games between the two sides were interrupted by rain and were quite dull affairs. By far the most exciting match was at Southampton in 1949. The county looked to have saved the game when they were dismissed in their second innings 108 runs ahead with only 45 minutes remaining. Most of the crowd made their way home, thinking the remaining time was largely academic. The tourists had other ideas. They knocked off the runs in 31 minutes for the loss of three wickets.

TOURED NEW ZEALAND

Only four Hampshire players have appeared in first-class cricket in New Zealand while on MCC/England tours: E.G. Wynyard (1906/07, captain), Chris Smith (1983/84), Robin Smith (1991/92) and Kevin Pietersen (2007/08). Wynyard's tour ended when he broke a tendon in his right leg while fielding in the second first-class match.

1,000 RUNS IN DEBUT SEASON

The only Hampshire player to register 1,000 runs in the season of his debut in first-class cricket was Harold Day. In 1922, aged 23, he scored 1,062 runs (average 39.33). The England selectors were sufficiently impressed to invite him to tour South Africa in the following winter, but being a serving officer in the Royal Artillery, he was unable to obtain leave.

SOME NICKNAMES

Nigel Cowley ....'Dougal'
Sean Ervine .... 'Slug'
Steve Malone ....'Piggy'
Raj Maru .... 'The Rat'
Tom Mottram...................................'The Pink Panther'
Chris Smith .... 'Kippy'
Robin Smith .... 'Judge'
Tim Tremlett...'Trooper'
Shaun Udal ....'Shaggy'

OLDEST PLAYER

The oldest player to appear for the county in a championship match was Henry Beauclerk Bethune. An army major, he was 52 years 188 days old when he played against Lancashire at Northlands Road in May 1897.

ODD INCIDENTS

There were several odd incidents in the match against Lancashire at Old Trafford in 1934. Between innings on the first day, the motor roller broke down and had to be hauled away from the centre of the ground. The wind was so strong on the last day that the bails were not used for long periods. A sightscreen was also blown down and broken.

JACK NEWMAN

John Alfred 'Jack' Newman would be high on any shortlist of Hampshire's best cricketers to be born in the county. He first saw the light of day at Southsea on 12 November 1884 and went to school at Bitterne in Southampton. He was first and foremost an off-break bowler with long tapering fingers and wonderful command of length, spin, flight and variations of pace. Throughout his career he deprived himself of many dismissals by refusing to bowl around the wicket and by his habit of running across the line of the stumps thereby unsighting the umpire when he appealed for leg before wicket. After the First World War, because Hampshire required it, he became a useful opening swing bowler. He would switch to his normal mode of delivery as the shine wore off the ball. Newman made his Hampshire bow in 1906. He claimed 100 wickets in a season on nine occasions, his best year being 1921 when he accounted for 177 batsmen (average 21.56). In this season he was the first player to perform the double of 1,000 runs and 100 wickets. He also recorded his highest score during the summer, 166 not out against Glamorgan at Southampton. Newman performed the double on five occasions between 1921 and 1928, the last being achieved when we was 44 years old. He was capable of touching inspired heights. He took a hat-trick against the 1909 Australians, captured 16 wickets for 88 at Weston-super-Mare in 1927, Hampshire's best match bowling figures, and hit two hundreds against Surrey at The Oval in the latter summer.

Newman's final wicket tally was 2,032 (average 24.20). Only two other players, George Dennett of Gloucestershire and Don Shepherd of Glamorgan, have taken over 2,000 wickets without playing for England. Like Alec Kennedy, he started his career batting at number 11, but by sheer application worked his way up the order to become a serviceable batsman who occasionally opened the innings. Newman was a sensitive man and following the 1930 season his health broke down aged 46. Though he returned to the first-class game as an umpire, his playing days were over. During the Second World War he went to live in Capetown where he became a highly popular coach. He died there on 27 December 1973 having made a final, nostalgic, return to Southampton's County Ground three years earlier.

OLDEST TEST DEBUTANT

Shaun Udal is Hampshire's oldest Test debutant. When he was selected against Pakistan at Multan in November 2005, he was 36 years 239 days old. Only three men have made their Test debut for England at an older age since 1945. Udal was also the oldest Englishman to make his first appearance against Pakistan. He had made his debut in ODIs over 11 years earlier.

OLDEST TEST PLAYER

E.G. Wynyard was 44 years 339 days old when he played against South Africa at the Old Wanderers, Johannesburg in March 1906.

OVER IN A DAY

Hampshire's match against Yorkshire at Southampton in 1898 was completed in a day. The first day was lost to heavy rain. Play started on the second at noon and ended at 6.05pm. In that time, Hampshire were dismissed for 42 and 36. Only one batsman, D.A. Steele, reached double figures (in the first innings). Schofield Haigh, making full use of the treacherous pitch drying out from the previous day's downpour, returned match figures of 14-43, hitting the stumps ten times. Yorkshire made 157 to win by an innings and 79 runs. The affair was a financial disaster for Hampshire's Harry Baldwin, as it was his benefit match.

THE JANE AUSTEN CONNECTION

The brothers Edward and George Knight, who played for Hampshire in the 1820s, were nephews of the novelist Jane Austen. Both were originally Austens but changed their name to Knight in 1812, in recognition of their father having been adopted, and inherited a large estate in Kent from their patron, Thomas Knight, some years earlier. George, through powerful and logical argument, played a significant role in the legalisation of round-arm bowling in 1835. A future Hampshire captain and president, Arthur Henry Wood, moved from his house in Alton to Chawton House, Chawton, which was owned by the Knight family, upon the death of his first wife towards the end of the 19th century.

UNITED SERVICES GROUND, PORTSMOUTH

No Hampshire ground was more susceptible to external influences than the United Services Ground in Burnaby Road. The omnipresent passing trains on the huge embankment at the Pavilion End were a constant feature. The growth of the trees at that end of the ground led to the postponement of county cricket in 1975. The county also did not play there in 1999 due to the poor quality of the wicket. The external environs of the ground were always changing as Portsmouth University developed the surrounding area. Another development was the creation of the indoor tennis area with its tent-like appearance in the Officers' Club sports complex. Many people will also recall the huge tractor roller which was a feature from just after the First World War. It ensured that the wickets in the late 1950s and 1960s were probably the hardest and fastest in the country, benefitting batsmen and bowlers alike. The inaugural first-class match at Burnaby Road occurred in 1882 when the Australians played Cambridge Past and Present, losing by 20 runs. The first Indian tourists, the Parsis, played two non first-class matches against the United Services in 1886. The Australians were regular visitors on their early tours and in 1893 ran up 843 against Oxford and Cambridge Past and Present. This was the highest innings total yet made in first-class cricket at the time and remained a ground record. The whole innings lasted only ten hours but continued until the third morning. The match was left drawn. Hampshire played their first match at Burnaby Road in 1887 against Sussex, which they lost by an innings.

The county were not then deemed to be first-class and so it was not until 1895 that Hampshire hosted championship cricket there. On that occasion they defeated Leicestershire by three wickets. Hampshire owed their victory to the bowling of the professionals Tom Soar (6-88 in the match) and James Wootton (7-78) and the batting of captain F.W.D. Quinton, who steered his team to victory with 55 not out in two and a half hours. As he had done at Northlands Road, Arthur Webb scored Hampshire's maiden first-class century at Portsmouth when he put together 111 against Sussex in 1897. Two years later, in his *annus mirabilis*, captain R.M. Poore became the only man ever to score a century in each innings on the ground when he made 104 and 119 not out against Somerset. The year of 1920 was one of records. In the inaugural match of Portsmouth's first cricket week, George Brown (151) and E.I.M. Barrett (148) added 280 for the second wicket against Warwickshire, as Hampshire totalled 616/7 declared – their highest innings total at Burnaby Road. The boot was on the other foot in the following match versus Yorkshire when Percy Holmes and Herbert Sutcliffe (131) added a ground record partnership of 347 for the first wicket. Holmes's 302 not out also remained a ground record. As if to emphasise the game's vagaries Hampshire were dismissed for just 35 in their second innings against Middlesex in 1922. Two years later Phil Mead and George Brown kept Yorkshire in the field until the second afternoon as they shared a Hampshire ground – and county – record third wicket partnership of 344. Mead scored most runs (5,155) and compiled most centuries (ten) there. Alec Kennedy was twice a thorn in Warwickshire's side in the 1920s. In the match already referred to he returned match figures of 12-147. His figures were even better in 1927. After even first innings totals (364-352) Kennedy turned the game on its head as he took 7-8 in ten overs on a drying pitch, his last six wickets coming in three overs at a cost of four runs. Warwickshire were to be on the receiving end of another record-breaking feat in 1960 when Derek Shackleton captured nine wickets for 30, dismissing the last six batsmen with the new ball in 26 deliveries without conceding a run. Shackleton always bowled well at Portsmouth; his 475 wickets there (average 18.34) were a ground record.

There was another phenomenal bowling performance at Burnaby Road a year later, when Butch White took four wickets, including a hat-trick, in the last over of the second day against Sussex to turn the match on its head and allow Hampshire to maintain their championship momentum next morning. Only Stuart Boyes (1925) and Lofty Herman (1937) had previously taken a hat-trick at Portsmouth. Jimmy Gray was another Hampshire player who prospered on the ground. In 1956 he became the first man to carry his bat there when he made 118 not out against Essex. Six years later he compiled 213 not out against Derbyshire – then the highest individual innings by a Hampshire player – at Portsmouth. Gray was on the field for the entire match; he made an undefeated 85 in the second innings when the rain came. The only tied match was against Middlesex in 1967. The previous encounter at Leicester had been drawn with the scores level and few could have anticipated another exciting game so shortly afterwards. Hampshire's performances at Portsmouth went a long way to securing the County Championship in 1973. Richard Gilliat played two captain's innings when making a century in each match, against Essex and Derbyshire respectively. Hampshire were more successful at Portsmouth than any other of their main grounds. They won 104 of their 315 matches there. Limited-overs cricket first came to Burnaby Road in 1965 when the county defeated Kent in a Gillette Cup match. The last matches at Portsmouth in 2000 provided more memorable occasions as Chris Tremlett made a startling entry into first-class cricket by taking a wicket with his first ball, and Shane Warne excited the crowds with his leg-spin bowling and his attractive batting. His absorbing day-long duel with Kent's Rahul Dravid in the last first-class match was a fitting finale.

THE PAKISTANIS

Between 1954 and 1992, Hampshire played the Pakistanis on seven occasions, winning once (in 1982) and losing once. The remaining five matches were drawn. The victory in 1982 at Bournemouth was noteworthy for a number of reasons. The match was originally arranged as Hampshire acceded to a request from the Test and County Cricket Board to fill a void in the Pakistan tour programme. In a match of declarations, Hampshire successfully chased 317 to win in 272 minutes for the loss of four wickets (Mark Nicholas 107 not out; Trevor Jesty 133).

Jesty had hit Abdul Qadir for 26 off one over. Qadir later bamboozled England's batsmen in the Test series. Robin Smith made his Hampshire debut (scoring eight and one). Hampshire's win was their first over a Test-playing touring side since they defeated the Indians in 1932. The match between Hampshire and the Pakistanis in 1987 earned notoriety because of a very public spat between the two captains, Mark Nicholas and Imran Khan, over a declaration. At the start of the third day, Nicholas was anxious to provide the crowd with an entertaining finish by declaring behind in the expectation that Imran would reciprocate with a subsequent declaration to set up an exciting run chase. Imran, though, wanted Hampshire to bat out their innings (they were 107 behind with six wickets in hand) so that he could test a bowling injury prior to the ensuing Test match. In the event, Nicholas declared at his side's overnight total and Imran eventually set a target of 318 in 49 overs. Hampshire batted out time and Imran did not bowl.

PAKISTANI OVERSEAS PLAYERS

Four Pakistanis have appeared for Hampshire in first-class cricket: Aaqib Javed in 1991, Wasim Akram in 2003, Imran Tahir (2008–09; 2011) and Sohail Tanvir (2013).

TOURED PAKISTAN

Those Hampshire players to have appeared in first-class cricket while with MCC/England sides are: Derek Shackleton (1951/52), David White (1961/62), Bob Cottam (1968/69), Kevin Pietersen and Shaun Udal (both in 2005/06). Peter Sainsbury and Udal toured there with England A sides in 1955/56 and 1995/96 respectively. White was the first Hampshire player to play in a Test against Pakistan on the above tour. His tour, and that made by Shackleton, included matches against India, and in the latter's case, Ceylon (as it was then named).

RUGBY INTERNATIONALS

Four Hampshire cricketers played international rugby: Cecil Abercrombie (six caps for Scotland from 1909–12); E.I.M. Barrett (one cap for Ireland in 1902); Harold Day (four caps for England from 1919–25); G.H.D. Lyon (two caps for England from 1907–08). Lyon later became Admiral Sir George Lyon.

NICK POCOCK

Hampshire's former captain and president as of 2013 remains county cricket's only Venezuelan-born participant. He was born in Maracaibo, where his father was an executive with Shell, in 1951.

PLAYERS OF THE YEAR

Since the introduction of this award in 1970, Hampshire's two great West Indian fast bowlers have been selected by their peers as the Professional Cricketers' Association Player of the Year – Andy Roberts in 1974 and Malcolm Marshall in 1982. Both were also nominated as one of *Wisden*'s Cricketers of the Year in their respective seasons.

FIRST CENTURY PARTNERSHIP

The first century partnership for Hampshire in first-class cricket was against Sussex at Hove in 1864: 101 for the seventh wicket between Henry Holmes (71) and George Ubsdell (29).

BARRY RICHARDS

Many who saw Barry Richards open for Hampshire between 1968 and 1977 will always regard him as the finest batsman they ever saw, or were ever likely to see. He was a genius of rare quality, a batsman who, with

TREVOR JESTY

assurance, could cut, late, from outside his leg stump to fine third man, or would dance down the wicket to bowlers of genuine pace and hit them straight, or back away to the leg side to any bowler and hit him anywhere on the off side. The latter ploy is common nowadays but Richards was the first to introduce, and perfect it. However, his technique was built on classic lines. Right-handed, tall, and broad-shouldered, he stood side-on and still as the bowler delivered the ball. He never moved until the ball was in the air. He therefore played his stroke very late which accounted for his almost wondrous timing. His off and cover driving were resplendent. Richards always made it look so easy. It was once observed that he could bat with a walking stick. More than any other batsman, he could drive crowds wild with hysteria through the sheer cheek and improvisation of his stroke play. Even experienced observers were heard to utter, 'Did you see that?' or 'Oh my word!' More often than not he was dismissed only when he decided he had had enough.

Richards's record shows that he overcame every hurdle, and usually at the first time of asking. He scored 2,000 runs in his first season in county cricket, 1,500 runs (including 300 in a day) in his only Australian season in first-class cricket, and 500 runs in his only Test series, incorporating one of the most masterful centuries ever seen in Test cricket. He predicted he would deliver a century in each innings against Kent at Southampton over Whitsun in 1976, one for his father's birthday and another for his mother's, and did so (159 and 108). He simply tore the Australian pace attack to shreds when composing 96 and 69 (retired hurt) in 1975. Richards carried his bat for 225 not out (out of 344) at Trent Bridge in 1974, and gave a master-class on a horribly difficult spinners' wicket with an undefeated 71 (out of 179) against Phil Edmonds and John Emburey of Middlesex at Northlands Road in 1975. As for one-day cricket, he set the standard for all batsmen. He eventually left Hampshire because he was simply bored with the routine. Like the prodigal son, he returned as president in 2009.

SENT OFF

Jack Newman was sent from the field by his captain, Lionel Tennyson, in the match against Nottinghamshire at Trent Bridge in 1922. On the second day Newman was being barracked by a section of the crowd for perceived time-wasting as he rearranged his field prior to bowling round the wicket. At the start of his next over Newman again painstakingly set his field, whereupon he incurred the wrath of the crowd once more. Newman expressed his displeasure by throwing the ball to the ground and stalking off away from the umpire's end upon completion of the over. Tennyson then intervened and instructed him to pick up the ball. Newman refused and Tennyson immediately ordered him off the field, an action for which there is no provision in the laws of cricket. The normally amiable Newman, who often shared racing tips with his captain, obeyed the order but kicked over the stumps en route to the pavilion, which he entered visibly upset. At the close of play, Tennyson stated that Newman's offence was using 'objectionable language'. Newman subsequently apologised to both Tennyson and the Nottinghamshire captain, Carr.

At the urgent request of the Hampshire committee, Tennyson permitted him to take the field on the resumption of play on the third day. However, Tennyson did not bowl him again during the remainder of the innings. Newman was rarely in good health during that summer. His actions may have been those of a very tired man who had for a moment completely lost his perspective.

RED CARD WITHDRAWN

Lionel Tennyson was involved in another sending-off incident. This time the circumstances involved a degree of comedy. In a match against Warwickshire at Southampton, a ball from Jim Bailey was played into the covers. Johnnie Arnold latched on to it and rifled a low return to the stumps at the bowler's end. Bailey thought about taking the ball but such was its speed, he withdrew his hand. The missile screamed to mid-on and delivered a blow to Tennyson's shin. He ordered Bailey off, feeling that the bowler should have stopped the ball before it reached him. Bailey reminded his captain that he had still to finish his over, and stayed on the field.

THE SOUTH AFRICANS

Between 1901 and 1994, Hampshire played the South Africans 13 times. They won the first encounter in 1901 and lost five, with seven draws. Because of South Africa's ban from international cricket the two sides did not meet between 1965 and 1994 and have not done so since the latter year. The 1901 fixture, which Hampshire won by an innings and 51 runs, was the South Africans' inaugural first-class match in England.

SOUTH AFRICAN OVERSEAS PLAYERS

The following South Africans have played for Hampshire: C.B. Llewellyn (1899–1910), G.B. von B. Melle (1914–21), Chris Smith (1980–91), Robin Smith (1982–2003), Stephen Jefferies (1988–89), Nic Pothas (2002–11), Kevin Pietersen (2005–10), J.J. McLean (2005–06), M. Hayward (2008), R.K. Kleinveldt (2008), Neil McKenzie (2010-date), J.G. Myburgh (2011), F. de Wet (2011). The Smith brothers qualified, and played for

England in Tests. Pothas and Myburgh were EU-qualified, McKenzie was a Kolpak registration, and Pietersen and McLean possessed British passports.

SOUTH AFRICAN TEST CRICKETERS

C.B. Llewellyn played in eight Tests while with Hampshire, and Richards four. Interestingly, Llewellyn was in England's squad of 14 prior to the Edgbaston Test against Australia in 1902 but was omitted on the morning of the match. The 11 that took the field is generally considered to be England's finest ever Test side. Richards's Test career was confined to one series against Australia in 1969/70 before being terminated when South Africa were banned after the end of that series. Richards had been named in the South African touring side to England in 1970; their place was taken by a Rest of the World team. Richards played five times for the representative side. The series was originally accorded as Tests but the status was later withdrawn. Hayward, Kleinveldt, McKenzie and latterly, Imran Tahir, all played with South Africa but not while they were with Hampshire.

TOURED SOUTH AFRICA

The following Hampshire players made Test tours to South Africa in MCC/England squads: E.G. Wynyard (1905/06 and 1909/10), Phil Mead (1913/14 and 1922/23), Lionel Tennyson (1913/14), Alec Kennedy, George Brown and Walter Livsey (all in 1922/23), Robin Smith (1995/96) and Kevin Pietersen (2009/10). Bob Cottam was selected for the MCC tour in 1968/69 which was cancelled in the wake of the D'Oliveira affair. The originally selected party toured Pakistan and Sri Lanka instead. Livsey returned home from the 1922/23 tour after damaging a hand without playing in a first-class match. Tennyson (as captain), Kennedy, and Tommy Jameson played in first-class matches on S.B. Joel's tour in 1924/25, as did David Turner on the D.H. Robins tour of 1972/73.

THE NOMADIC IMRAN TAHIR

Has there ever been a more nomadic cricketer than Imran Tahir? In his 14-year career to date, he has played for 17 teams in first-class cricket – nine in his native Pakistan, four in England and four in South Africa, for whom he has now played Test cricket. He has also appeared for four other counties in second XI cricket as well as for sides in the Lancashire League, and the North Staffordshire and South Cheshire League.

SUBSTITUTIONS

Hampshire's first substitution occurred in 1914. The South African Basil Melle received a telegram at Trent Bridge recalling him for army service, as the First World War had started a few days earlier. Although he had bowled a few overs, the Nottinghamshire captain allowed Jimmy Stone to take Melle's place and bat in his stead. It was the only such instance in Hampshire's history until 2005 when Chris Tremlett, made 12th man in England's side at Lord's, replaced Billy Taylor in the match against Sussex at the Ageas Bowl. The latter had previously bowled four overs. Tremlett, batting at 11, scored 44 not out in Hampshire's second innings, sharing in a match-changing tenth wicket partnership of 83 with Nic Pothas. Later on in the season, Tremlett replaced James Bruce at Cheltenham in similar circumstances. Bruce had taken 3-42 in 12 overs by the time his team-mate arrived. The only other instance was Michael Lumb replacing Marcus North in 2009. There have been a number of cases of Hampshire calling up reserve wicketkeepers during the course of a match, but they have never been allowed to bat.

RUNNERS-UP (2) ROBBED BY RAIN

County Championship table 1974:

	P	W	L	D	NR	Bt	Bw	Pts
Worcestershire	20	11	3	6	0	45	72	227
Hampshire	20	10	3	6	1	55	70	225
Northamptonshire	20	9	2	9	0	46	67	203

Hampshire were unequivocally robbed of a second consecutive championship title by the rain. When they overwhelmed Worcestershire by an innings and 41 runs in two days at Portsmouth on 8 August, they had established a lead of 31 points over that county. Each had five games to play. However, rain then intervened crucially in four of those five remaining games. The equivalent of a full day's play was lost in the next match, against Lancashire at Bournemouth with Hampshire in an unassailable position. However, they took six bonus points to Worcestershire's four and were therefore 33 points ahead with four matches to go. The next encounter was against Glamorgan at Cardiff. On a slow pitch, Hampshire eked out 234 before Andy Roberts took seven wickets in an amazing display of pace and cunning to leave Glamorgan at 43/7. Heavy rain on Sunday left a wicket so soft and spongy that their opponents were just able to avoid the follow-on. By now, the drying pitch was a sticky turner of which, despite a near miraculous 60 by Barry Richards, the Glamorgan bowlers took full advantage. On a true wicket Glamorgan squeezed home by five wickets. Hampshire totally dominated the return at Southampton, hitting 393 later in the week, but rain again intervened, washing out play for all but 15 minutes on the second day. Hampshire needed to take 17 Glamorgan wickets on the final day for an innings victory; they took 15. Rain then washed away the final day of the next match against Somerset at Bournemouth with Hampshire needing to take the final six wickets and Somerset requiring 52 runs to avoid an innings defeat. By now, Worcestershire had registered three wins and were only two points behind Hampshire as each county entered their last match. Hampshire never even took the field against Yorkshire at Bournemouth. Rain ensured the match was abandoned without a ball being bowled. In the meantime, there was sufficient play at Chelmsford for Worcestershire to secure four points and the championship. Rain had therefore washed out six of the 15 days in Hampshire's matches since the counties met at Portsmouth. In three of five matches it almost certainly prevented the county from achieving victory. Hampshire had headed the table since early June. Though three matches were lost, the team was immeasurably stronger than in 1973. Four of the ten victories against Kent, Nottinghamshire, Sussex and Worcestershire were by an innings in two days. Essex were also defeated by an innings and Hampshire completed another two-day win at Northampton. The ace in the pack was the West Indian Andy Roberts. He took 111 championship wickets at an average of only 13.45. He was ably supported by Bob Herman (70 wickets) and Mike Taylor (63). Barry Richards headed the batting averages with 1,059 runs (average 55.73), including 225 not out from 344 all out at Trent Bridge. However, it is the intrusive and destructive rain over these last three weeks of the season that will endure.

FIRST TRIPLE CENTURY

The cricket world was agog with the news of the sport's first triple century in August 1874. Batting for Northwood against Freshwater at Cowes, Isle of Wight, W.E.W. Collins struck 338 not out. Although considered a very good club cricketer, Collins played little at first-class level. He was a noted author.

KEVIN PIETERSEN

Hampshire supporters revelled in Kevin Pietersen's headlong batting in his debut ODI series in South Africa in early 2005. He scored 454 runs at more than a run a ball, including three centuries. He had already signed for the county for the 2005 season. However, it became increasingly difficult for Hampshire supporters to identify with him because they saw him so rarely. After his thrilling Test debut against Australia at Lord's in 2005, he played only one first-class match for the county, at Taunton in

2008. Just to emphasise what the Hampshire faithful had been missing, he hit 100 not out. He also played for the county in List A matches on only 17 occasions in all. While he is technically Hampshire's most capped player in Tests, ODIs and Twenty20 internationals, that fact must be accompanied by a postscript.

HAMPSHIRE'S ROLL OF HONOUR

The following men who had played for Hampshire were killed in the First World War: C.H. Abercrombie, A.C. Arnold, F.H. Bacon, G. Belcher, C.H. Bodington, E.R. Bradford, G.M.L. Brodhurst, A.M. Byng, A.G.S. Garvie, T. Gregory, J.H. Gunner, A. Jaques, R.W.F. Jesson, C.H. Palmer, H.W. Persse, H.J. Rogers, G.A.C. Sandman, C.N. Sutcliffe, G.P.R. Toynbee, K.H.C. Woodroffe.

Hampshire cricketers who lost their lives in the Second World War were F.G.B. Arkwright, J.P. Blake, N.H. Bowell, A.K. Campbell and D.F. Walker.

NORTHLANDS ROAD, SOUTHAMPTON

Hampshire's association with Northlands Road dated from 1883 when the secretary, Colonel James Fellowes, opened negotiations with the Hulse Estate for the lease and development of a new ground off Bannister Road. In January 1884 Colonel Fellowes was able to report that eight acres had been leased at a cost of £169 per year on the condition that a pavilion was built. The ground was vested in eight trustees and a guarantee fund of £2,000 was established for its development. The ground was officially opened on 9 May 1885, at a grand bazaar which accompanied the first game played there, between North Hampshire and South Hampshire. The first county match was not arranged until 15 June, when MCC were the visitors. It proved to be an inauspicious beginning as Hampshire were soundly beaten by an innings and 113 runs by lunch on the second day.

Two more innings defeats, at the hands of Derbyshire and Surrey, and another reversal against Kent ensued in the next month. Hampshire's fortunes then took an upward turn in August. They recorded the first victory at their new home when they overturned Sussex by 101 runs and towards the end of the month beat Somerset, who played throughout with only nine men, by eight wickets. However, the county were deprived of their first-class status at the end of the season and did not regain it until they were admitted to the modern County Championship in 1895. Despite this considerable setback the club continued to develop the ground. In 1886 a new wing was added to the pavilion for the professionals' use. A concrete wicket was also laid. In the following year a groundsman, Tom Soar, was appointed. He was the first of a loyal, and relatively short, line of dedicated men to have lovingly tended the ground. In 1887 the highest innings ever recorded on the county ground was played. F.E. Lacey, who was later to become secretary of MCC and the first man to be knighted for his services to cricket, scored 323 in four and a half hours against Norfolk. Hampshire celebrated their re-entry to the County Championship in 1895 in the grand manner by thrashing Derbyshire by an innings in two days. Soar and the tubby Harry Baldwin were the heroes. They bowled unchanged in both innings to return match figures of 11-113 and 8-93 respectively. The following year was notable for two significant innings. Captain E.G. 'Teddy' Wynyard pounded the Yorkshire attack to the tune of 268 as Hampshire reached 500 for the first time at their headquarters. Only determined resistance by the Yorkshire tail prevented a memorable Hampshire victory. An even larger innings was played by the Somerset opening batsman, Lionel Palairet. He elegantly charmed his way to 292 in six and a half hours. His score was only bettered when Graeme Hick hit a largely inexperienced Hampshire attack for 303 not out in the final match of the 1997 season. Hick's innings is the highest ever played against Hampshire and his undefeated partnership of 438 with Tom Moody was a ground record. Harry Baldwin's benefit match against Yorkshire in 1898 provided the only instance of a Hampshire match being completed in a day. The years from the turn of the century to the First World War produced three outstanding performances against touring sides.

The South Africans played their first match in England at Southampton in 1901. They were overwhelmed by an innings as one of their fellow countrymen, Charles Llewellyn, punished their bowling for 216 before taking six wickets and three catches. Later in the year, Llewellyn, who was the first of Hampshire's outstanding array of overseas players, dismissed 14 Worcestershire batsmen for 171 to register what was the best match return at Southampton. In 1909 Jack Newman took a hat-trick against the Australians. Three years later Hampshire notched their first victory over the auld enemy. The foundations were laid by the immovable Philip Mead who scored 160 not out in the first innings. Alec Kennedy ensured they stayed on the rack as the county emerged victors by eight wickets. During the years immediately following the First World War the county ground was a batsman's paradise. Twice in 1919 over 600 runs were scored in a day's play. The following year George Brown and E.I.M. Barrett shared a second wicket stand of 321 against Gloucestershire, the highest partnership by a Hampshire pair on the ground. In 1921 Mead hit the Nottinghamshire bowling for an unbeaten 280, eclipsing Wynyard's effort of some years earlier. This score remained unsurpassed by a Hampshire player at Southampton in first-class cricket. It was also no surprise that

Hampshire's most prolific batsman registered the most number of runs at the county ground – 14,504. In the same year, the formidable Australians made the largest innings total. Thanks to a double century by Bardsley and further hundreds by Taylor and Macartney they were able to declare at 708/7. Hampshire though were not overawed and replied honourably with 370 (Mead 129), the best score by a county against the Australians all summer. The orgy of run-scoring continued in 1923. Middlesex's total of 642/3 declared was compiled with the help of four centurions. Yet another record was established the following year. Kennedy interrupted the batsmen's monopoly when he took eight Gloucestershire wickets for 24, including a hat-trick. Kennedy went on to take the most wickets by any bowler at Northlands Road – 606. Kennedy's inseparable partner, Jack Newman, was not far behind with 542. Two of the most famous batsmen in the game achieved 1,000 runs before the end of May at Southampton. Walter Hammond was the first in 1927. Later in the match Lionel Tennyson smashed the fastest century at Southampton, racing to his century in just 55 minutes. Donald Bradman emulated Hammond in 1930 and 1938.

It was in 1950 that Southampton staged its closest match when the traditional Whitsun encounter with Kent ended in a tie. Hampshire's highest innings total, 600/8 declared against Sussex in 1990, was compiled with the help of David Gower who scored 145 on his championship debut for the county and Robin Smith's 181. While less memorable cricket was seen at the county ground after the advent of four-day championship cricket, there were still a few highlights, none more so than Cardigan Connor's 9-38 against Gloucestershire in 1996, the best innings figures at Northlands Road. Memories of one-day cricket will be defined by three World Cup matches (one in 1983 and the other two in 1999), as well as a succession of disappointing semi-final appearances in the major one-day competitions. Northlands Road had always been a hoodoo ground and it was not until 1992, when Hampshire defeated Somerset in the semi-final of the Benson and Hedges Cup, that the spell was broken.

YORKSHIRE AT SOUTHAMPTON

Almost incredibly, until 2006, Hampshire had never beaten Yorkshire at either Northlands Road or the Rose Bowl. At their 25th attempt they completed a comprehensive ten-wicket victory at the latter ground. Moreover, having beaten Yorkshire at Headingley earlier in the season, the victory also meant that Hampshire completed their first double in the same summer over that county in 112 years of championship cricket.

HAMPSHIRE'S MOST DESTRUCTIVE BOWLER

Who was Hampshire's most destructive bowler? Using the yardstick of balls per wicket, it was the leg-spinning all-rounder Harold Clark McDonnell, who played 78 times from 1908–1921. He took 263 wickets at a strike rate of 36.72. He had previously played for Surrey and Cambridge University. Being a schoolmaster at Twyford School he only appeared for Hampshire during the school holidays. The county's official history commented that 'he was a magnificent fielder to his own bowling, expected to catch the hardest drives hit back at him, often did so, and was furious when he didn't'. Those bowlers who have taken over 150 wickets for the county with the best strike rate have been: H.C. McDonnell 36.72; J.R. Badcock 43.19; A.M.E. Roberts 43.87; M.D. Marshall 45.53; H.V. Hesketh-Prichard 45.53; C.B. Llewellyn 46.98.

STRANGE GOINGS-ON (2)

In 1908, the second day's play between Hampshire and Sussex at Priory Park, Chichester, was abandoned without a ball being bowled. However, the bald fact masks some strange occurrences. After the previous day's play had also been abandoned, K.S. Ranjitsinhji invited his team-mates to Shillinglee Park, an estate he was renting 22 miles away. The majority accepted. The next morning the umpires inspected the pitch and decided play could start at 11.30am as scheduled. They sent a telegram to Shillinglee at 10.15am with the news. However, at it was still heavily raining at Shillinglee, Ranji took no notice. It was only when two further telegrams were received that it became apparent to him the match was ready to commence. Hampshire had been present at the scheduled start. The two Sussex players who were not staying on Ranji's estate were also waiting on the ground. Prompted by the communications, C.B. Fry and Joe Vine arrived at 12.30pm, but Ranji and the other six players did not arrive until 3.30pm. By 4.15pm all the Sussex team were ready to take the field but more heavy rain then made any play impossible on the day. Hampshire captain E.M. Sprot would have been perfectly within his rights to claim the match but chose not to do so. Though there was a full day's play on the next day, the match was inevitably drawn. Ranji made partial recompense for his arrogance by entertaining the crowd with an unbeaten 51. He did not escape entirely unscathed from the incident. He earned a rebuke from Lord's following MCC's receipt of a report on his shenanigans.

DEREK SHACKLETON

Derek Shackleton was one of those rare cricketers who became a legend during his playing career. Even upon his death in 2007 almost 40 years after his final game for Hampshire, his name remained synonymous with accurate line and length bowling. 'Shackleton-like' became a simile for accuracy. His team-mates averred that upon inspection of the pitch, after his bowling spell, which invariably was a long one, there was a bare patch about the size of a plate, on a length. He rarely visited the nets but once, at Southampton, he bowled three balls which hit off, middle and leg stumps consecutively. Just to prove it was no fluke he bowled a further three balls and hit the stumps in reverse order.

Shackleton, though, was never given to ostentation, except perhaps in his dapper attire. He went about his work quietly and apparently tirelessly. He never seemed to take much out of himself, which is perhaps why he lived to 83, an old age for a pace bowler. However, he took enough. The body action and follow-through lifted him off the ground and batsmen testified to the ball hitting further up the bat than they expected. He was tall, just over 6ft, lean and spare in build, with never a hair out of place. By the end of his career he ran to the crease off just six full strides. His wrist was cocked in the delivery stride and his inordinately long sinewy fingers gave him total ball control. After each delivery there was a habitual two-handed hitch of the trousers. Shackleton bowled a fuller length than contemporary bowlers, giving the ball opportunity to swing. He was able to deviate it late both ways. Colin Cowdrey, and others, found it difficult to detect the direction of his swing while the ball was airborne. Cowdrey, Ted Dexter and Ken Barrington, three indisputably great batsmen, were in awe of his accuracy. There were no looseners; Shack hit a length from the first ball. He was virtually un-hittable. Fred Trueman, the most aggressive of batsmen, enjoyed some success by hitting him 'on length'. Shackleton always applauded any batsman who hit him for six. Top-order batsmen, though, even those of the highest class, rarely succeeded in unsettling him. His skill and economy became the benchmark against which all of his successors have been judged. Shackleton's statistics are mind-boggling and, like Philip Mead's run scoring, created their own miscellany.

DEREK SHACKLETON MISCELLANY

He joined Hampshire as a batsman, who bowled leg-spinners, and captured a record 2,669 wickets for the county.

He took 100 wickets in a season in 20 consecutive summers (1949–1968), a record for any bowler. Yorkshire's Wilfred Rhodes passed the 100-wicket landmark 23 times, but not in successive seasons.

Apart from 1953, Shackleton headed the Hampshire bowling averages in every season from 1950 to 1967.

His first-class tally of 2,857 wickets has been bettered by only seven bowlers, one of whom is Alec Kennedy (2,874).

He took 1,497 wickets in the 1950s, equal with Yorkshire's Johnny Wardle and bettered only by Surrey's Tony Lock.

MORE SHACKLETON

He claimed 1,239 wickets in the 1960s, behind only Middlesex's Fred Titmus.

Shackleton bowled more overs than any other bowler in seven seasons (1956, 1957, 1958, 1961, 1962, 1963 and 1966). He reached the age of 42 during the last of these years.

He was the season's leading wicket-taker on five occasions – 1959, 1962, 1963, 1964 and 1965 and was the first to 100 wickets in 1962 and 1964.

He captured nine wickets in an innings four times, the most by a Hampshire bowler.

In 1955, Shackleton returned the remarkable figures of 11.1 overs, seven maidens, four runs, eight wickets against Somerset at Weston-super-Mare. He took 6-25 in 16 overs in the second innings, to finish with a match analysis of 14-29.

When he was recalled to the England side to play the West Indies at Lord's in 1963, it was 11 years 230 days and 103 Tests since his previous appearance. He took three wickets in four balls to end the West Indies' first innings and retained his place for the rest of the series.

THE SRI LANKANS

Between 1981 and 1998, Hampshire played the Sri Lankans on five occasions. The Sri Lankans won the last match with four draws. Highlights were Gordon Greenidge captaining Hampshire for the only time and Richard Hayward scoring 101 not out on his debut in 1981, Robin Smith scoring 132 and 97 in 1984, and Aravinda de Silva making 221 not out in 1990.

SRI LANKAN OVERSEAS PLAYERS

Two Sri Lankans have played for Hampshire in first-class cricket: W.P.U.J.C. (Chaminda) Vaas in 2003, and H.M.R.B.K. (Rangana) Herath in 2010. In the latter year, Ajantha Mendis was the original overseas selection but Herath took his place.

TOURED SRI LANKA

Robin Smith became the first Hampshire man to appear in Test cricket in Sri Lanka when England toured there after playing in India in 1992/93. Derek Shackleton (1951/52) and Bob Cottam (1968/69) played first-class matches there for MCC on wider tours of the Indian sub-continent. Mark Nicholas (captain), Chris Smith and Tim Tremlett played with England B in 1985/86.

INTERNATIONAL FOOTBALLERS

Eight Hampshire cricketers played international football for England: John Arnold (one cap), Ted Drake (five), C.B. Fry (one), L.H. Gay (three), E.B. Haygarth (one), A.E. Knight (one), L.V. Lodge (one), and G.B. Raikes (four). Arnold, Fry and Gay were double internationals, having also played cricket for England. However, only Arnold was a Hampshire player at the time of making his international appearances in both sports. Fry was with Sussex and Gay with Cambridge University and Somerset when they played football for England.

MARRIED TO ALICE

The Hampshire cricketer Reginald Gervis Hargreaves is notable for marrying Alice Liddell, the girl upon whom Lewis Carroll based his 'Alice' in the world famous book. Hargreaves was born in Accrington and played 12 matches for the county between 1875 and 1885. Both he and Alice are buried in the churchyard at Lyndhurst, the town in which they spent their married life.

THE ANTELOPE GROUND, SOUTHAMPTON

The Antelope Ground was the headquarters of Hampshire cricket from 1839 to 1884. From 1864, when the county played their first match as Hampshire County Cricket Club, until the latter year, Hampshire played 27 matches, won 11, lost 13 and drew two. The ground played host to some notable firsts: first win as a first-class county in 1865, defeating Surrey by eight wickets; first century scored for Hampshire, CF Lucas's 135 v

Surrey in 1866; first visit by an Australian side to Hampshire in 1880, they defeated Eighteen of Hampshire by an innings in their opening match of the tour in three hours. The best bowling performance for Hampshire on the ground was 8-57 by Cecil Currie against Somerset in 1882. However, it was Derbyshire's William Mycroft who recorded the best figures. He claimed 9-25 and 8-78 in 1876, and yet finished on the losing side as Hampshire sneaked a one-wicket victory. The highest score at the Antelope was by Francis Lacey, who scored 211, as well as 92 not out in the second innings, against Kent in 1884. That year was their last on the ground. It was ironic that Hampshire should reserve their best performance for their final match there, against Somerset. They amassed 645 (Lacey 100 and E.O. Powell 140) and won by an innings and 169 runs.

Hampshire's departure to the County Ground in Northlands Road wasn't quite the end of the Antelope Ground as a sporting venue. Southampton FC played there in their formative years from 1887 until 1896 when they then moved temporarily to the County Ground, prior to their transfer to The Dell. By the first decade of the new century, the Antelope Ground had been built over and all remaining vestiges of the ground, located along St. Mary's Road, were swept away by German bombs in the Second World War.

HAMPSHIRE'S FIRST BOWLING MACHINE

Bowling machines are generally assumed to be a relatively modern invention, but one was first seen in Hampshire as long ago as 1844. In a match at Southampton's Antelope Ground 'Eleven players of the County of Hampshire' took to the field against 'Thirteen gentlemen of the South Hants Club, with the Catapulta'. The gentlemen had only to bat and field, for all the bowling was performed by the machine. The Catapulta was devised by Nicholas Felix, the great Kent player of the period. It was based on the Roman siege machine. It seemed to possess most of the attributes of the current appliance of the modern bowling machine. The length, direction and speed of the ball could all be varied by adjusting the machine. The match, played over two innings on a single day, was drawn.

LIONEL TENNYSON

Many cricket writers dubbed Lionel Tennyson 'Regency Buck', a man born out of his time. He was arguably cricket's most colourful character of the 20th century. He was a hard-hitting batsman with a penchant for smiting sixes. His courage was a by-word. The faster the bowling the more he was at home. In 1921, he batted in a Test match one-handed against the two fastest bowlers, operating in tandem, that the world had yet seen, and hit them time and again to the boundary. He scored 63 and 36, as well as holding a brilliant overhead catch. He captained England in the last three Tests of that series and was Hampshire's longest serving skipper. He always led from the front. He became England's finest ambassador as the then developing countries, notably the West Indies, were establishing their cricket foundation.

Some of the game's most endearing and colourful stories emanated from his on-field and dressing room antics. Tennyson's off-field exploits would have been a godsend to today's tabloids. It was often said that he did not always behave in the manner expected of a peer of the realm. In his day the newspapers were more discreet, which for him was just as well. With his chaotic private life, prodigious appetite for the high life and substantial gambling losses, the modern journalist would never have lacked a story. Tennyson would have been permanent headline news had he lived today. In the First World War, he saw action in all the main battles, was wounded three times and twice mentioned in despatches. He was, though, never decorated, almost certainly because of a high-profile divorce case. The last few years of his life were a sad decline but he had already lived the equivalent of several lives. In 1951, he died in bed, reading his newspaper, aged 61. Players in the Test between England and South Africa at Trent Bridge stood in silence in his honour.

TENNYSON STORIES

Tennyson was fond of sending telegrams to his batsmen. After winning the toss in a match with Middlesex he wrote out the batting order and retired to take a long bath. When he eventually emerged he glanced at the scoreboard, only to find that the innings was progressing far too slowly. He then summoned a messenger and dictated a telegram to one of the procrastinating batsmen, none other than Philip Mead. It read, 'Too slow. Get out at once. Tennyson.' During Bournemouth week, Tennyson would often seek a doubles partner for a tennis match. On one occasion, he instructed his fledgling partner to lose the first set, which they duly did. Their opponents then increased their wager. Almost needless to say, Tennyson and his by now streetwise accomplice proceeded to win the match and claim the spoils. The same tennis partner was once walking around the ground with his captain, now Lord Tennyson, when they noticed a spectator was walking haphazardly in front of them. Tennyson exclaimed, 'He's had one too many!' His companion, perhaps making a Freudian slip, promptly replied, 'One too many! He's as drunk as a lord.' Tennyson was stopped in his tracks.

DOUBLE BLUE AT CRICKET AND RUGBY

A.H. Evans obtained a cricket Blue at Oxford in the four seasons between 1878 and 1881. He gained his rugby Blue in 1877 and 1878. He was also a noted athlete. Alfred Henry Evans played three matches for the county in 1885. He had previously represented Somerset. He founded a cricketing dynasty. Two sons and three nephews also played for the county.

RUNNERS-UP (3)

After 1974, Hampshire have been runners-up twice in the County Championship, in 1985 and 2005. In the first of those years, which was Mark Nicholas's first as captain, they finished 18 points behind a very fine Middlesex side. Going into the final match they were only one point behind their rivals. However, Middlesex beat Warwickshire by an innings while Hampshire could only draw at Trent Bridge. As in 1974, Hampshire cursed the rain. It robbed them of certain wins over Yorkshire and Lancashire while in the match against Kent they finished three runs short of victory in a thrilling run-chase. However, in the key match against a weakened Middlesex at Dean Park, the visitors' last two batsmen held out for 29 overs to force a draw. It was the defining moment of the season. In 2005 Hampshire were 2.5 points behind Nottinghamshire. The decisive moment was when Nottinghamshire clinched the championship in their penultimate match at Canterbury. With time lost to rain and a Kent win vital if they were to retain any hope of the title, the two captains engineered a finish whereby Kent required 420 runs to win from 70 overs. They were bowled out for just 205. Hampshire were due to play Nottinghamshire in their last match. Shane Warne was incandescent about the contrivance. 'I think that's one of the dumbest things I've ever seen,' he said. Nottinghamshire fielded a weakened side at the Rose Bowl and were duly thrashed in three days by an innings and 188 runs. Hampshire had also recorded a three-day victory over them earlier in the season. On that occasion Chris Tremlett claimed a hat-trick to set up the win. A large contributory factor to the success was their winning six of their eight home matches. It was a fine team effort as Hampshire had to compensate for the absence of Warne for five matches while he was on Australian tour duty.

MARK NICHOLAS

Hampshire were phenomenally successful under Mark Nicholas's captaincy. A championship eluded him, though the second place in 1985 (see above), and a third in 1990 were still meritorious achievements. Despite the presence of the great Malcolm Marshall, the county were always a bowler short during Nicholas's tenure. He also led the county to Sunday League success in 1986. However, he will always be remembered for leading Hampshire to their first three Lord's finals, all of which were won. He was unable to play in the second, against Surrey in 1991, because of a hand injury. His captaincy was directly instrumental in Hampshire defeating Derbyshire in the first in 1988, and he took a miraculous catch to keep his side in control in 1992. His other great contribution was to retain the confidence of the indomitable Marshall. Their friendship was strong, and when Marshall died in 1999, his former captain delivered two memorable and evocative eulogies at his funeral in Barbados and a memorial service in St. Mary's Church in Southampton. He skippered Hampshire to victories over India in 1990 and the West Indies in a one-day game in 1995, and came tantalisingly close to toppling the Australians in 1985 and 1993. Nicholas also captained two England reserve sides to Sri Lanka in 1985/86 and Zimbabwe in 1989/90. As a batsman, he was an almost casual stroke maker. Two centuries against Australia were a benchmark of his quality. Hundreds against all the counties, except Middlesex and Warwickshire, demonstrated his adaptability. Nicholas always performed with panache and style and brought these qualities to bear in his latter career as television commentator and anchorman, and writer.

TEST MATCH FRINGES

Famously, Chris Tremlett was England's 12th man in the first four Tests of the pulsating Ashes series in 2005. Neville Rogers (against South Africa at The Oval in 1951) and Peter Sainsbury (two Tests v New Zealand in 1958) were also England's 12th man. Bob Parks was a stand-in wicketkeeper on the Saturday of the Lord's Test v New Zealand in 1986. Both David Turner (v West Indies at Edgbaston in 1973) and Adam Rouse (v Sri Lanka at the Ageas Bowl in 2011) fielded for England. Rouse entered the record books by catching Kumar Sangakkara off Jimmy Anderson.

ROBIN SMITH

Robin Smith left the county at the end of the 2003 season with a formidable legacy. His statistics are contained elsewhere in this book but they give no indication of the excitement of his stroke play. His walk to the wicket bristled with intent. He blinked his eyes to become accustomed to the light as he emerged from the pavilion. Then, approaching the wicket in a businesslike manner, he wielded his bat in a wide circle alongside his head, first with one hand and then the other. He then exercised each wrist with bat in hand. On reaching the wicket he kicked away the loose earth in his crease. On a dry pitch the wicketkeeper and surrounding close fielders almost required a face mask as they became enveloped in a dust cloud. After taking guard he then blinked his eyes again and flexed his knees as he bent down and sprang from his haunches. It is one of the wonders of physiology that he never suffered an injury during this series of callisthenics. Smith waited for quick bowlers in the bat up position, taking minute stuttering steps across the wicket to bring him into line of the stumps. He picked his bat up straight and played further forward and back than any batsman of his generation. His trademark was the most brutal of square cuts and his driving through extra cover was the litmus test of his form. He always played off his legs through mid-on and midwicket with certainty. Smith's bravery was a byword. The enduring memories will be his two centuries for Hampshire against the Australians. In 1993, with his Test place under considerable pressure, he dominated their bowling and struck a thunderous 191 at a run a ball. No fewer than 152 of those runs were scored in boundaries. On a gloriously sunny Sunday he scored 136 runs before lunch. In terms of context and the quality of the opposition, it was one of the greatest innings ever played at Northlands Road. Eight years later, at the Rose Bowl, Smith led Hampshire to a famous victory, during the course of which he struck another hundred. This was a more mellow innings. There were odd glimpses of his power but, with the reflexes now slower, he battled his way to a century in a manner which the Australians respected. He stoically took blow after blow and literally batted himself to a standstill in making 113. The innings showed that time had not diminished his relish for the fight.

SHAUN UDAL

On his championship debut at Arundel in 1990, Hampshire-born Shaun Udal looked the part immediately. Skilfully nursed by Mark Nicholas, his development was rapid. A hernia restricted his appearances to one-day matches only in 1991 but he ended the season with a Benson and Hedges Cup winner's medal. Two years later, he returned career best figures with eight Sussex wickets for 50 at Southampton. Given the admiration expressed by Ray Illingworth, the new chairman of selectors, it was unsurprising that he was promoted to the ODI side against New Zealand and South Africa in 1994. He was duly selected for the winter tour to Australia. Unfortunately, he broke a finger in the first match at Lilac Hill, and then pulled a rib muscle, an injury that was to plague him for several years. Nevertheless, on his return, he enjoyed another good summer and was chosen for a further three internationals against the West Indies. However, he missed out on the winter tour to South Africa, and then fell further down the England spin-bowling pecking order on a disappointing A tour to Pakistan. Though his batting improved – he recorded a cherished 117 not out against Warwickshire at Northlands Road in 1997 – his bowling fell away. His appointment as vice-captain halted the slide. With the move to the Rose Bowl the luxury of bowling into Alan Mullally's footmarks, and the captaincy and shrewd field placings of Shane Warne, enabled Udal to became a force once more. His performance in that famous victory over the 2001 Australians when he single-handedly carried Hampshire's bowling attack for virtually four sessions, with the temperatures above 90 degrees, spoke volumes for his character. And so his career moved to its unlikely climax. He captained the county in the C&G Trophy win against Warwickshire at Lord's in 2005, and received a call-up for the winter tours of Pakistan and India. He made his England debut in the first Test against Pakistan at Multan, and retained his place for the rest of the series. Illness ruled him out of the early part of the ensuing tour to India but he gained his place in the sun when he bowled England to an unlikely victory at Mumbai. The iconic moment was the dismissal of Sachin Tendulkar, with the classic spinner's wicket – a bat/pad catch to short leg. It proved to be Udal's last Test. After his sad departure from Hampshire in 2007, he extended his Indian summer by captaining Middlesex to the Twenty20 trophy in the following summer, ironically at the Rose Bowl.

HAMPSHIRE UMPIRES

	Career	Matches
J. Arnold	1951, 1961–72	275
H. Baldwin	1907–09	59
G. Brown	1935–36	45
W.L. Budd	1969–84	268
N.G. Cowley	1996–2013	193
P.J. Hartley	2002-2013	132
O.W. Herman	1963–74	211
R.S. Herman	1979–82	60
J.W. Holder	1982–2009	421
H. Holmes	1883–1899	110
H. Horton	1973–76	73
T.E. Jesty	1993–2013	268
S.J. Malone	2008–11	6
J.A. Newman	1931–39	219
A.E. Pothecary	1949–58	255
D. Shackleton	1979–81	50
J. Stone	1912, 1925–34	236
B.V. Taylor	2012-2013	3
J.J. Tuck	1886–99, 1908	90
F.G. Willoughby	1906	21

HAMPSHIRE'S ONLY TEST UMPIRE

John Holder is Hampshire's only Test umpire. He officiated in 11 Tests between 1988 and 2001. He also umpired in 19 ODIs, including five in India and five in Sharjah in the UAE. Fittingly, the final match of his umpiring career was in a NatWest Pro40 match at the Ageas Bowl.

COUNTY CRICKET IN WINCHESTER

In 1875, in an attempt to generate interest outside of Southampton, the county scheduled two matches in Winchester. The first was against Sussex at the Green Jackets Ground at St. Cross. The other was at the Winchester College ground, where Kent were the visitors. Hampshire were heavily defeated in both matches by an innings in two days and the experiment was not repeated. *Lillywhite's Cricketer's Companion* uncharitably referred to the second match as 'a mere farce'. Hampshire made only 34 and 82, while Kent piled on 333. The county had fared little better a few weeks earlier when they restricted Sussex to 206, but were then bowled out for 60 and 119.

UNIVERSITY BACKGROUNDS

Until well into the 20th century an Oxbridge Blue for cricket was often a passport for a place, usually as a batsman, in a county side. Fifty-five men with Oxford and Cambridge Blues have appeared for Hampshire. However, with the accent on academic work, and with Oxbridge degrees being the prelude to earning a fortune in the financial and legal centres of the world, that well has dried. The last two cricketing Blues to play for Hampshire on leaving Oxford were Richard Gilliat and Will Kendall (Blue 1995/96; Hampshire debut 1996). Apart from John Crawley, who came to Hampshire after a distinguished career with Lancashire, no Cambridge Blue has played for the county since Chris Goldie in 1983. The modern cricketer emanates from a very different university as the list below of players who have made their debut for the county since 2000 demonstrates:

Loughborough – Jimmy Adams, Chris Benham, John Francis

Durham – Charlie van der Gucht, John Francis, Michael Brown, James Bruce, Mark Thorburn, David Balcombe

Bradford – James Schofield

West of England – James Hamblin

Cardiff – James Tomlinson

Southampton Solent – Tom Burrows

SHANE WARNE

The great Australian leg-spinner galvanised Hampshire from the moment he stepped on to the field at Chelmsford for the first time in 2000. When he returned to Hampshire in 2004, as captain, they gained promotion to Division One of the championship and finished third in the National League. His bravado and confidence rubbed off on the other players. As a consequence they displayed new self-belief. The opposition were confronted with a set of new and very different demands, not only arising from his bowling but also his field placings, which were invariably designed to take wickets rather than prevent runs. He had introduced, and imposed, a completely different mindset for his own players and Hampshire's opponents. He never spared himself in Hampshire's cause. Warne's workload and commitment were on a par with another great, Malcolm Marshall. There can be no higher praise. He still continues to visit the Ageas Bowl, which possesses a stand bearing his name, when he is in the country.

VICTORY AFTER FOLLOWING ON

Hampshire have won three matches after following on:

1895 – Taunton, won by 11 runs
Somerset 221 (L.C.H. Palairet 96, A.E. Clapp 60 not out; H. Baldwin 5-62, T. Soar 4-87) and 176 (Soar 7-71)
Hampshire 94 (S.M.J. Woods 6-48, E. Tyler 3-46) and 314 (F.H. Bacon 92, H.F. Ward 71, Tyler 6-117)
This was Hampshire's very first match after being admitted to the County Championship. Somerset required only 45 runs to win with five wickets in hand at the start of the third morning. However, they lost those wickets, four of them to Tom Soar, for just ten runs as Hampshire achieved a dramatic victory.

1922 – Birmingham, won by 155 runs
Warwickshire 223 (F.R. Santall 84, F.S.G. Calthorpe 70) and 158 (J.A. Newman 5-53, A.S. Kennedy 4-47)
Hampshire 15 (H. Howell 6-7, Calthorpe 4-4) and 521 (G. Brown 172, W.H. Livsey 110 not out)
This match has legendary status. But for Tennyson's streaky boundary via a dropped catch in the slips, Hampshire could have been dismissed for 11. Mead was six not out having middled every ball. In their second innings, Hampshire were still 31 in arrears when their sixth wicket fell on the stroke of lunch on the second day, at 177. George Brown then masterminded one of cricket's great comebacks as he added 95 with Bill

Shirley (30) and 177 for the ninth wicket with Walter Livsey. The latter recorded his maiden century. A deflated Warwickshire were then routed by Kennedy and Newman on the final day.

2003 – Rose Bowl, won by 93 runs

Glamorgan 437 (A. Dale 123, M.P. Maynard 124) and 104 (C.T. Tremlett 6-51)

Hampshire 185 (M. Kasprowicz 5-48) and 449 (N. Pothas 121, A.D. Mascarenhas 75, R.J.E. Hindley 68 not out, S.M. Katich 53, R.D.B. Croft 5-117)

The Times felt that the win 'was scarcely less dramatic' than that at Birmingham 81 years earlier. When Simon Katich was dismissed off the last ball of the second day, Hampshire were 114/4, still 138 runs in arrears. Nic Pothas, handicapped with a hamstring injury, then reprised George Brown's role by shepherding the lower order, adding 149 for the sixth wicket with Mascarenhas. Richard Hindley, a 28-year-old left-handed batsman from Southern League Havant, who had been drafted in to the side as an off-spin bowler to replace the injured Shaun Udal, played heroically. He sustained two broken fingers while forestalling the Glamorgan bowlers in his only appearance for the county. Chris Tremlett's then career best sealed a remarkable win.

THE WEST INDIANS

Between 1906 and 1995, Hampshire played the West Indians 14 times. They won the first two in 1906 and 1923, but then lost five and drew seven. Highlights were Hampshire's W.T. Langford recording eight for 82, the best analysis in matches between the sides, in 1906; Lionel Tennyson scoring a rumbustious 217 and sharing 313 with Jack Newman (118) in 1928; C.B. Clarke (6-32 and 7-75) spinning the West Indies to a ten-wicket victory at Bournemouth in 1939; Roy Marshall stroking 135 for the West Indies on his first appearance in Hampshire, only to be upstaged by Everton Weekes who plundered 246 not out on the same day when the West Indies scored 539/4 on a day when the crowd was so large that the boundaries were shortened continually to accommodate them; West Indies hanging on grimly at 128/9 as Hampshire pressed for victory against one of the finest of all touring sides in 1963; West Indies scoring 397/7 to win by three wickets in 1969; a typically belligerent 176 by Viv Richards in his halcyon year of 1976; simply sublime centuries by Carl Hooper – 196 and 195 – in 1991 and 1995 respectively and in the latter innings, he struck ten sixes.

WEST INDIAN OVERSEAS PLAYERS

The following West Indians have played for Hampshire: Roy Marshall (1953–72), Danny Livingstone (1959–72), Gordon Greenidge (1970–87), Andy Roberts (1973–78), Malcolm Marshall (1979–93), Elvis Reifer (1984), Linden Joseph (1990), Winston Benjamin (1994–96), Nixon McLean (1998–99), Daren Powell (2009) and Ruel Braithwaite (2013). Greenidge came to Reading from his native Barbados at the age of 14, and could have opted to play for England. Livingstone was born in Antigua, completed his education in Canada and became qualified living in Warwickshire while serving in the RAF. Milton Small was the original choice to replace Marshall in 1984, but he was then selected for the West Indies tour party. Reifer, who had never played first-class cricket before, subsequently took his place.

WEST INDIAN TEST CRICKETERS

Hampshire followers took great pride in the performances of their three stellar West Indians in Test cricket in the 1970s and 1980s. Greenidge played in 87 Tests while with Hampshire, Malcolm Marshall 81 and Roberts 27. Marshall's entire Test career was as a Hampshire player. McLean (four) and Benjamin (five) also appeared for the West Indians during their stints with the county. Roy Marshall had played in four Tests prior to joining Hampshire. Powell never played in a Test during his brief spell.

TOURED THE WEST INDIES

The only two Hampshire men to make England Test tours of the West Indies are Robin Smith (1989/90 and 1993/94) and Kevin Pietersen (2008/09). Jimmy Adams and Danny Briggs participated for England Lions with marked success in the West Indies' domestic first-class competition in 2011/12. George Brown (1910/11), Arthur Jaques (1912/13) and Lionel Tennyson and Tommy Jameson (both 1925/26) all visited the islands on MCC first-class tours. A host of Hampshire players have also played in the islands on minor tours in first-class cricket. These include E.G. Wynyard, H.V. Hesketh-Prichard, Phil Mead, Desmond Eagar, Colin Ingleby-Mackenzie, David Blake, Roy Marshall and Alan Castell.

THE WICKETKEEPERS

Hampshire have fielded only 12 regular wicketkeepers since their admission to the County Championship in 1895:

	Matches	Ct	St	Total
C. Robson 1895–1906	129	165	37	202
J. Stone 1900–14	274	361	113	474
W.H. Livsey 1913–29	309	375	254	629
G. Brown * 1908–33	539	484	51	535
N. McCorkell 1932–51	383	512	176	688
L. Harrison * 1939–66	387	567	99	666
B.S.V. Timms 1959–68	208	402	60	462
G.R. Stephenson 1969–80	263	570	75	645
R.J. Parks 1980–92	253	630	70	700
A.N. Aymes 1987–2002	215	516	44	560
N. Pothas 2002–11	132	375	23	398
M.D. Bates 2010–date	39	120	5	125

* The figures for George Brown and Leo Harrison include catches in the field.

FIVE STUMPINGS IN AN INNINGS

George Ubsdell was Hampshire's first regular wicketkeeper in first-class cricket. In the county's sixth match, he established a record that is unlikely to be beaten when he stumped five batsmen in Surrey's second innings at The Antelope Ground in 1865. All of the dismissals were off the slow right-arm bowling of James Southerton, who went on to play for England in the inaugural Test against Australia in March 1877. Southerton was then a Surrey player. Ubsdell played 15 matches for Hampshire between 1864 and 1870, dismissing 17 batsmen behind the wicket, of whom 13 were stumped. He later moved to Lancashire, where he became groundsman of the Aigburth ground in Liverpool.

MOST VICTIMS IN AN INNINGS

Nic Pothas achieved the record when he caught seven batsmen in Lancashire's only innings at Old Trafford in 2006.

MOST VICTIMS IN A MATCH

Three wicketkeepers hold this feat with ten dismissals: Bob Parks (v Derbyshire at Portsmouth in 1981), Adi Aymes (v Oxford University at The Parks in 1989) and Nic Pothas (v Durham at Chester-le-Street in 2008).

MOST DISMISSALS IN A SEASON

Leo Harrison claimed this tally when he dismissed 83 batsmen (76 caught, seven stumped) in 1959. Harrison's number of catches in that season is also a record. The most dismissals in a season since 1993 is 58 by Nic Pothas (56 caught, two stumped) in 2006.

MOST STUMPINGS IN A SEASON

Walter Livsey created the Hampshire record when he stumped 32 batsmen in 1921. Livsey stumped more than 20 batsmen in a season on nine occasions. The only other wicketkeeper to perform the feat was Neil McCorkell (31 in 1932).

NO BYES

In 1938, wicketkeeper Neil McCorkell did not concede a bye during Leicestershire's marathon 535/8 declared at Aylestone Road, Leicester. The Hampshire bowlers sent down 976 balls during the course of the innings.

NIC POTHAS

When *Wisden Cricketer* commissioned Sussex's Robin Martin-Jenkins to select the best county team of the first decade of this century, Nic Pothas was his nomination as wicketkeeper. The latter had stood expertly to the leg-breaks and googlies of Shane Warne and Imran Tahir, left-armer Alan Mullally's pace movement, Chris Tremlett's speed, Shaun Udal's off-spin and the slow left-arm spin of Danny Briggs. He therefore had to cope with virtually all of the bowlers' variations and did so admirably. His figures justifying him as Hampshire's best ever wicketkeeper/batsman are difficult to ignore. As for his batting, no cause ever felt lost while Pothas was at the wicket. He had to be prised out. He always retained the priceless asset of keeping the scoreboard ticking. This trait was exemplified in Hampshire's miraculous win, after following on, over Glamorgan at the Rose Bowl in 2003 when he piloted the comeback with 121, batting on one leg. Similarly, Hampshire's record eighth wicket partnership of 257 was also conceived from a seemingly hopeless situation. After subsiding to 83/7 before lunch at Cheltenham, Pothas, in company with Andy Bichel, turned the match around. Pothas intelligently played second fiddle to the Australian's pyrotechnics but moved remorselessly to his own century. He was dismissed shortly before close of play for 139. But for injury, he would undoubtedly have reached the much coveted 1,000 runs in a season on five occasions. As it was, his season's aggregate of 973 runs in 2005 and 2006 was the best by a wicketkeeper for over 50 years. He averaged over 50 in a season four times, his best being an eye-watering 74 in 2009.

His mannerisms were ingrained in the minds of Hampshire supporters. Pothas was one of the game's most assiduous fidgets. After reinforcing his guard, he became an inveterate sweeper of creases, first in front of the line and then behind, and then sometimes more than once each. After tugging at his box, the peak of his helmet and his gloves, he awaited the bowler in a bat up position. He was a fine judge of what ball to leave alone or what to play. He defended resolutely early on, but as he became accustomed to the pace of the pitch, he began to unfurl his attacking shots. He drove powerfully and pulled and hooked with some relish. If he had been able to qualify for England earlier he must have played Test cricket. He was a cricketer of considerable stature.

ADI AYMES

Adi Aymes played in two finals at Lord's. He first appeared for a losing Hursley Park in the National Village Cup Final in 1984. Seven years later he claimed a winner's medal in the NatWest Trophy Final when Hampshire defeated Surrey.

WISDEN CRICKETERS OF THE YEAR

Sixteen Hampshire players have been nominated in *Wisden*'s annual list of their Five Cricketers of the Year, for their performances in the preceding season. No player can win the award more than once. Only those who were Hampshire players at the time of their nomination are listed.

1900 R.M. Poore; 1911 Charles Llewellyn; 1912 Phil Mead; 1914 Lionel Tennyson; 1933 Alec Kennedy; 1959 Roy Marshall and Derek Shackleton; 1969 Barry Richards; 1974 Peter Sainsbury; 1975 Andy Roberts; 1977 Gordon Greenidge; 1983 Trevor Jesty and Malcolm Marshall; 1984 Chris Smith; 1990 Robin Smith; 2006 Kevin Pietersen. Gordon Greenidge received his nomination for his performances with the touring West Indies.

The following players were similarly nominated by *Wisden* before or after they were contracted to Hampshire: David Gower (1979), Shane Warne (1994), Dominic Cork (1996), Matthew Hayden (2003), Ian Harvey (2004), Neil McKenzie (2009) and Michael Clarke (2010). Shane Warne was nominated as one of *Wisden*'s Five Cricketers of the Century in 2000.

YOUNGEST CENTURION

The county's youngest centurion is Liam Dawson. He was 18 years 211 days old when he made 100 not out against Nottinghamshire at Trent Bridge on 27 September 2008.

YOUNG CRICKETER OF THE YEAR

Since its inception by the Cricket Writers' Club in 1950, two Hampshire players have won this annual award. Colin Ingleby-Mackenzie was selected in 1958 and Bob Cottam in 1968.

YOUNGEST DEBUTANT

The youngest ever debutant in county cricket was Charles Robertson Young, who was 15 years 131 days old when he took the field for Hampshire against Kent at Gravesend on 13 June 1867. An amateur and left-handed all-rounder, he went on to play 38 matches for the county until 1885.

YOUNGEST DOUBLE CENTURION

Barry Richards became Hampshire's youngest double centurion when he struck 206 against Nottinghamshire at Portsmouth in 1968. He was 23 years 38 days old.

HAMPSHIRE'S YOUNGEST ENGLAND DEBUTANT

The above honour goes to John Arnold. He was 23 years 209 days old when he played against New Zealand at Lord's in 1931. It was to remain his only Test appearance.

ZIMBABWE

Hampshire played one match against Zimbabwe in 2000, which was drawn. It was the last game against a touring side at Southampton's former County Ground.

ZIMBABWEAN OVERSEAS PLAYERS

The following Zimbabweans have played for Hampshire: Heath Streak (1995), Neil Johnson (2001–02), Greg Lamb (2004–08) and Sean Ervine (2005–date). Ervine is the holder of an Irish passport and therefore played for the county by virtue of an EU qualification.

TOURED ZIMBABWE

Mark Nicholas (captain), Bob Parks and Paul Terry toured Zimbabwe with an English Counties side in 1984/85. The tour was in jeopardy at one stage as the Zimbabwean government banned Nicholas and two other players because they had previous cricket connections with South Africa, who were barred from the world stage at the time. However, the tour manager, Mike Vockins of Worcestershire, made it clear the tour would not take place if the prohibition stayed in place. The Zimbabweans blinked first and the restriction was lifted. Nicholas also captained an England A side in 1989/90.

LIST A SECTION – INAUGURAL MATCH

Hampshire's first match was against Derbyshire at Bournemouth in the Gillette Cup in May 1963. They lost an exciting 65-over game by six runs. Derbyshire, after being invited to bat, stuttered to 149/6 before Derek Morgan (59 not out) and Bill Richardson (39) added 63. With ten runs coming off the last over, Derbyshire closed at 250/9. Hampshire's response was built entirely around Mike Barnard. Going in at the fall of the first wicket, he was last out for 98, attempting a big hit three balls before the end. Morgan won the man of the match award. Barnard was given a special award of a silver medal, the only Hampshire player ever to receive one. Hampshire fielded eight batsmen, one genuine all-rounder (Peter Sainsbury), and only two specialist bowlers (Butch White and Alan Wassell). Denis Baldry and Jimmy Gray were the fill-in bowlers. Colin Ingleby-Mackenzie also kept wicket in lieu of Bryan Timms. Four Hampshire batsmen were run out, three of them at the end of the innings.

MIKE BARNARD

Footballer/cricketer Mike Barnard commented in a radio interview a few years ago that his game was more suited to one-day cricket as he lacked the concentration to convert fifties into hundreds. This is certainly borne out by his stats as he scored 46 fifties but only six centuries. However, an indication of his quality was that he scored three of those hundreds against touring sides. Two of them were especially meritorious. His maiden century of 101 not out against Pakistan at Portsmouth in 1954 was on a slow, seam bowler's wicket on which the next highest score by any batsman on either side was 47. His final hundred was a splendid 123 against Australia at Southampton ten years later which only just failed to bring victory. Perhaps, though, his two best innings were in the championship summer of 1961. With Hampshire precariously placed in their first innings, he stroked a magnificent 114 not out in 155 minutes against Warwickshire at Southampton to turn the tide. Then, in the match versus Derbyshire at Bournemouth when Hampshire clinched the title, his partnership of 99 in only 68 minutes with Peter Sainsbury (73), enabled Hampshire to declare with sufficient time to bowl out their opponents. The feature of the partnership was their running of what seemed non-existent singles. Barnard made 61.

A PLAY ON NAMES

In Hampshire's Gillette Cup tie at Chippenham in 1964, two Wiltshire players with the same names as two of Hampshire's greatest batsmen colluded to dismiss Peter Sainsbury. He was caught Richards bowled Marshall.

THE MINOR COUNTIES

Between 1964 and 2005, Hampshire played teams from the Minor Counties Championship in 25 matches in the Gillette Cup, NatWest Trophy and C&G Trophy, and won them all. They also possessed a 100 per cent record against Minor Counties South (3-0) in the Benson and Hedges Cup. They did, however, suffer a reversal against the Minor Counties Cricket Association (MCCA) at Southampton in 1981, losing by three runs. Hampshire won their other three matches against the MCCA.

SAINSBURY TOUR DE FORCE

In taking 7-30 against Norfolk at Southampton in 1965, Peter Sainsbury returned the best bowling figures for Hampshire in List A matches. Having earlier scored 76 in Hampshire's innings, he won the match of the match award, the first Hampshire player to do so. His all-round performance is also still the best in such matches. Sainsbury won the man of the match award again in the following match against Kent at Portsmouth, when he scored 70 and claimed 3-45 in his allowable 13 overs.

LOSING SEMI-FINALISTS (1)

In 1966, after defeating Lincolnshire, Kent and Surrey, all at home, Hampshire reached their first semi-final. However, they were trounced by Worcestershire at New Road by 99 runs. The home side batted first, scoring 253/4 (Martin Horton 114 not out). Hampshire replied with 154. The unfortunate Butch White was wicketless while conceding 89 runs in ten overs. It is still the most expensive analysis by a Hampshire bowler. The match was the start of a long road to Lord's.

FIRST CENTURY

Roy Marshall made Hampshire's first List A century with 102 against Lincolnshire at Basingstoke in 1967. While he was run out, 12 of the 18 batsmen who were dismissed in the match were clean bowled.

MAN OF THE MATCH FOR FIELDING

Barry Reed scored 47 while sharing an opening partnership of 110 with Roy Marshall (61) when Hampshire defeated Glamorgan by 16 runs in their Gillette Cup tie at Portsmouth in 1967. He went on to win the man of the match award for this innings and 'his excellent fielding at cover'.

BARRY REED

Barry Reed's career was an interesting one. He played in one match in 1958 but then, partly upon his father's advice and also because of a long-term injury that took years to heal, he went to work in the City. His interest was rekindled after watching the first Gillette Cup Final in 1963. By this time, he was married and living in Brighton. He duly wrote to both Sussex and Hampshire. Much to his astonishment, he received a reply from Desmond Eagar, the Hampshire secretary, informing him that the county still retained his registration. He joined the Hampshire staff as a non-contracted player in 1965 and retained this status until his last match in 1970. He did not therefore start a full-time career in the game until he was almost 28. The diminutive right-handed opening batsman started making up for lost time on his return by scoring five half-centuries in his first nine innings. He batted consistently as he proved an ideal foil to the fast-scoring Roy Marshall and Barry Richards, but retired upon the advent of Gordon Greenidge. By now, he was a farmer, but continued to make a huge contribution to Hampshire by serving on the cricket committee and managing the Hampshire Under-19 side for many years.

MOST APPEARANCES

In a career from 1968 to 1989, David Turner made 377 List A appearances for Hampshire. He is followed by Shaun Udal (356), Robin Smith (347) and Mark Nicholas (346).

MOST RUNS AND CENTURIES

Robin Smith has scored the most List A runs (12,034) and most centuries (23) for Hampshire. Given the reduction in the number of List A matches each season, these records may well stand the test of time. David Turner made 9,835 runs (five centuries) and Gordon Greenidge 9,801 runs (20 centuries).

RUNNERS-UP IN THE INAUGURAL SUNDAY LEAGUE

The John Player (Sunday) League 1969:

	P	W	L	NR	Pts
Lancashire	16	12	3	1	49
Hampshire	16	12	4	0	48
Essex	16	11	4	1	45

Hampshire finished as runners-up in the inaugural Sunday League, sponsored by John Player which was of 40 overs per side. The county were one of the main proponents for the introduction of a limited overs league and responded accordingly. The chase for the title was a three-horse race virtually all season. With four matches to play, Hampshire had to visit Lancashire at Old Trafford and then host Essex at Portsmouth. Before a massive crowd of 12,500, the county accounted for the eventual winners by 48 runs. However, before a record Portsmouth crowd estimated at 8,000, they then lost to Essex by 24 runs. Batting first Essex made 195. Hampshire responded with quick runs at the top of the order but the dismissal of Barry Richards (65) in the 22nd over, with the score at 108, proved decisive. The county fell behind the run rate and the tail collapsed spectacularly in their efforts to make up lost ground. The final six wickets fell for just 12 runs. Despite then winning the last two matches, Hampshire fell just short of the ultimate goal. Their performances throughout the season captured the imagination and the team drew a substantial audience throughout. Barry Richards (405 runs) invariably ensured an attractive start. Richard Gilliat (333 runs), captain Roy Marshall (336 runs), who moved himself to four in the batting order, as well as Danny Livingstone, who hit ten sixes in the summer, enabled the middle order to maintain momentum. Peter Sainsbury captured 28 wickets to demonstrate that spin bowlers would always have a place in limited overs cricket. Remarkably, at the age of 45, Derek Shackleton headed the bowling averages and conceded only 37 runs per 100 balls. Butch White took 5-31 in his benefit match against Yorkshire at Southampton. Bob Cottam and Trevor Jesty also enjoyed productive seasons. The fielding was splendid throughout. Richards held 12 catches and 14 of the opposition batsmen were run out. Wicketkeeper Bob Stephenson, often standing up to the quicker bowlers, made four stumpings, as well as holding 13 catches. Surprisingly, rain interfered in only one match, at Northampton, which was reduced to 32 overs per side.

DANNY LIVINGSTONE

West Indians seem to trade in exotic christian names but surely the Antigua-born Daintes Abbia Livingstone tops them all. Always known as Danny, he was an integral member of Hampshire's championship side in 1961 and he earned immortality as the man whose outfield catch sealed the title. He was an attractive batsman who was able to give free rein to his hitting prowess in the early years of the Sunday League. Left-handed, of medium height and stockily built, his best innings for Hampshire was undoubtedly a breathtaking 151 against the West Indian tourists at Southampton in 1963. He came to the wicket after both Roy Marshall and Jimmy Gray had been dismissed for five in the first six overs. Undaunted, he scored his runs (18 fours and two sixes) out of 245 while he was at the wicket. It was the highest innings against the redoubtable tourists all summer. The start of his career best 200 against Surrey at Southampton a year earlier has entered into Hampshire lore. Prior to receiving his first ball from Tony Lock, he failed to notice David Sydenham sitting among the crowd at long leg. He promptly hoisted the ball straight to where the latter was now standing but Sydenham dropped it. He and Alan Castell (76) went on to post a Hampshire record 230 for the ninth wicket. Livingstone's most lasting legacy is possibly the most important development in West Indian cricket. Upon his retirement he returned to his native Antigua to become coach and then selector and manager of the Leewards and Combined Island teams. He performed all these tasks so proficiently that within the next few years Viv Richards, Andy Roberts, Richie Richardson, Curtley Ambrose and Winston Benjamin from Antigua and Keith Arthurton from Nevis rolled off the production line. It was a far cry from the situation that applied in 1963 when he played his most famous innings against a West Indies side that did not include a single player from the Leeward Islands. He died on 8 September 1998 aged 54.

RUN OUT WITHOUT FACING

With Barry Richards absent due to injury, Keith Wheatley received a late call to join the Hampshire team for their Gillette Cup tie at Old Trafford in 1970. He opened the innings and was run out without facing a ball.

INAUSPICIOUS START FOR RICHARDS AND GREENIDGE

When Barry Richards and Gordon Greenidge opened the innings for the first time in a List A match at Edgbaston in 1970, the former was dismissed in the first over with the total still at 0. Greenidge made only five. They had batted together in the previous Sunday League match against Glamorgan at Southampton, adding 74, but on that occasion Greenidge batted at three in the order. They went on to record ten century partnerships for the first wicket, the highest of which was 220 (unbeaten) against Nottinghamshire at Southampton in 1977. Two years earlier, they had put on 210 against Glamorgan at Southampton.

SOBERS SECOND TO SAINSBURY

Besides being one of the greatest batsmen of all time, it is often forgotten that Gary Sobers was a formidable left-arm fast-medium swing bowler. He was irresistible in a Gillette Cup tie at Portsmouth in 1971. He reduced Hampshire to 7/3, his victims being Richards (0), Greenidge (4) and David Turner (2). He later bowled Trevor Jesty and finished with figures of 4-11 off 12 overs, half of which were maidens. Notwithstanding Sobers's attentions, Hampshire, requiring 130, eased home by three wickets with five overs to spare. Sobers was also beaten to the man of the match award by Hampshire's much more unheralded all-rounder, Peter Sainsbury. On his 37th birthday, Sainsbury received the award from adjudicator Bill Edrich for his patient batting (he top scored in Hampshire's innings with 32), fine fielding and economical bowling (conceding only 22 runs in his 12 overs). It was not often that Sobers took second place to another all-rounder.

LONG JOURNEYS

For many years Sunday League matches were played during a three-day match which started on the previous day. One recurring complaint from players was the distances they were required to travel for their Sunday game after completion of Saturday's play. When Hampshire played Gloucestershire at Portsmouth in 1971, they had come from Westcliff and their opponents from Gloucester. The distances were 120 and 100 miles respectively. Both teams, of course, then had to make the return journey upon completion of the Sunday match. For the record, Hampshire lost by 67 runs.

MARSHALL DISMISSED BY SHACKLETON

Julian Shackleton, son of Derek, made his debut for Gloucestershire in the aforementioned match. He took 2-47, one of his wickets being his father's long-term team-mate Roy Marshall.

LESS RUNS BUT WON

In a Sunday League match at Bournemouth in 1971, Hampshire were still 28 runs short of Yorkshire's total of 202 when stumps were drawn at the scheduled time of 6.30pm. However, the visitors, captained by Geoffrey Boycott, had bowled only 34 overs instead of the allotted 40. Hampshire therefore won by virtue of a faster run rate – 5.17 to Yorkshire's 5.05.

FIRST BENSON AND HEDGES CUP MATCH

Hampshire played their inaugural Benson and Hedges Cup match in 1972 in the unlikely surroundings of the Cotswold market town of Moreton-in-Marsh. The match was originally scheduled for Saturday 6 May but there was no play because of rain. On the Sunday, Hampshire travelled to Edgbaston for a Sunday League match against Warwickshire. When play started on Monday, it was again interrupted by rain, and the match was not completed until Tuesday. Hampshire made 169 and then dismissed Gloucestershire for 70. Bob Herman's 4-42 earned him the man of the match award.

LOWEST INNINGS TOTAL

After Essex had made 172, Hampshire were bowled out for 43 on a difficult, drying pitch at Basingstoke in the Sunday League in 1972. It remains the county's lowest total in List A matches. Only captain Richard Gilliat (14) made double figures. The last five wickets fell in 25 balls without a run being scored. Surprisingly, six Essex bowlers shared the wickets.

RECORD PARTNERSHIP

After Barry Richards had been dismissed with the score at 36, Gordon Greenidge (173 not out) and David Turner (123 not out) batted through the rest of the innings in adding 285 runs in 150 minutes against Minor Counties South at Amersham in 1973. It remains Hampshire's highest partnership for any wicket in List A matches.

IAN BOTHAM ANNOUNCES HIS ARRIVAL

Hampshire were on the receiving end of Ian Botham's first heroic effort in the Benson & Hedges Cup quarter-final at Taunton in 1974. Hampshire batted first and ran up 182, mainly thanks to a fifth wicket stand of 95 between Trevor Jesty (79) and Peter Sainsbury (40). Botham (2-33 in 11 overs) broke the partnership and had earlier bowled Barry Richards. With Jesty taking four wickets, Somerset then subsided to 113/8, needing 70 off the last 15 overs. A Hampshire victory seemed a formality. Botham had other ideas. Batting at nine, he scored 45 not out to bring Somerset home by one wicket with an over to spare. At one stage, he was felled after a bouncer from Andy Roberts was deflected from his glove onto his mouth. Botham spat out fragments from two teeth, drank a cup of water, and carried on batting. It almost goes without stating that he won the man of the match award. A legend had been born.

LOSING SEMI-FINALISTS (2)

Hampshire's form in limited overs cricket in 1975 was their most assured to date. They played with complete certainty and command. They cruised through the group stages of the Benson & Hedges Cup, winning all their matches, and then defeated an excellent Somerset side in the quarter-finals. Unfortunately, the wheels came off in the semi-final at Leicester. On a slow pitch, designed to nullify the pace of Andy Roberts, Hampshire batted first. They lost the wicket of Richards in the first over and never recovered from the blow. As the shrewd captaincy of Ray Illingworth imposed a stranglehold on the Hampshire batsmen, Gordon Greenidge played a lone hand with a quite magnificent 111 before being seventh out with the score at 186. Only Richard Gilliat (22) and Peter Sainsbury (26) provided any support. Requiring 217, Leicestershire won by five wickets with five balls to spare. Roberts bowled very fast indeed, taking 1-16 in 65 balls. However, the Leicestershire batsmen concentrated on keeping him out and targeted the other bowlers. The tactic worked as Chris Balderstone (101 not out) and Roger Tolchard (38) took the midland county to victory. The most memorable feature of their innings was Tolchard's phenomenal running between the wickets. He had played for Hampshire's second XI earlier in his career.

HIGHEST INNINGS

Gordon Greenidge hammered 177, the highest individual innings for Hampshire in a List A match, against Glamorgan in a Gillette Cup clash at Southampton in 1975. He and Barry Richards (129) had added 210 for the first wicket. Greenidge was the junior partner during the stand but after the South African's dismissal, he launched his own onslaught. He hit seven sixes. Hampshire's total of 371-7 also remains a county record. Hampshire sauntered to victory by 164 runs, yet another record for them in List A matches against a first-class county.

FIRST ONE-DAY TROPHY

Hampshire's first triumph in a one-day competition was in the Fenner Trophy at Scarborough in 1975. The county were invited to participate in the famous Scarborough Festival by virtue of their array of fast-scoring batsmen, who would appeal to the holiday crowds. Four teams participated in a 50-over competition. In their first match, they defeated Gloucestershire by 87 runs. They ran up 290, with man of the match Richard Gilliat scoring 124, before dismissing their opponents for 203, Mike Taylor taking 3-33. The final against hosts Yorkshire turned into a duel between the two star opening batsmen on each side. Geoff Boycott made 116 in Yorkshire's 240/6 but Barry Richards replied with an unbeaten 106 to see his side home by seven wickets with four overs to spare. However, matches in the Fenner

Trophy and the other one-day competitions in the Scarborough Festival are not recognised as List A matches.

HAMPSHIRE AT SCARBOROUGH

Hampshire's popularity was such that they were invited to return to Scarborough Festival time and again. They continued to be successful. They won the Fenner Trophy in 1975, 1976, 1977 and were joint winners in 1980, the Asda Cricket Challenge in 1984 and 1986, the Scarborough Festival Trophy in 1990 and were joint winners of the Joshua Tetley Festival Trophy in 1992. They also won the Tilcon Trophy at Harrogate in 1976.

MOST WICKETS

Cardigan Connor (411) has taken the most wickets in List A matches. He is followed by Shaun Udal (407) and Trevor Jesty (334).

SUNDAY CHAMPIONS (1)

John Player (Sunday) League table 1975:

	P	W	L	Pts
Hampshire	16	13	3	52
Worcestershire	16	12	3	50
Kent	16	12	4	48
Essex	16	10	6	40

Hampshire claimed their first List A trophy when they won the John Player League in 1975. It was a closely fought competition throughout. After losing to their main rivals Worcestershire in the first match, the county then recorded five successive victories to take them to the top of the table. However, they then lost the lead to Essex after two defeats in the next three matches. Thereafter, they were unstoppable as they registered a record seven straight wins. All those matches included noteworthy highlights. First, Gloucestershire were despatched by four wickets with time to spare after Barry Richards and Gordon Greenidge plundered 138 at indecent speed. A limping Greenidge then thumped 102 off only 67 balls (five sixes and five fours) in 87 minutes at Weston-super-Mare. Andy Roberts smashed a tremendous last-over six as Hampshire scraped home by two wickets with one ball remaining at Bradford. The ensuing match against Northamptonshire at Southampton then threatened to thwart the county's ambitions. Rain had left a sodden outfield but the umpires eventually sanctioned a ten-overs-a-side match. John Rice's hat-trick, the first for the county in the competition, effectively settled the issue. The final three matches were televised. Hampshire defeated Essex by 98 runs at Chelmsford before thrashing Leicestershire by six wickets. Richards treated the record Bournemouth crowd to a virtuoso display as he toyed with the bowlers, stroking 112 (five sixes and 12 fours), in 74 minutes, in just 25 overs. Even the canny Ray Illingworth was reduced to impotence. Hampshire chased down their target of 195 in only 29.2 overs. It was revenge of sorts for the semi-final defeat in the B & H Cup (see page 109). The final match of the campaign was at the little village ground at Darley Dale in Derbyshire. Richards (52) and Greenidge (55) gave Hampshire an initial advantage which they never relinquished. Tom Mottram (5-21) and John Rice (4-14) ensured the landmark victory by 70 runs. Richards dominated proceedings throughout with a then record 689 runs (average 45.93). Six bowlers, led by Rice (27 wickets) took 11 wickets or more.

JOHN RICE

Chandler's Ford-born John Rice joined Hampshire in 1971 after a year on the Surrey staff and made his first-class debut immediately as a right-arm medium pace bowler. After starting his career at number ten in the order, through careful thought and application, he became a serviceable opening batsman. His bowling always remained an invaluable asset particularly in limited overs matches. He was an integral member of the Hampshire team in both of their first two Sunday League championships in 1975 and 1978. He was also a fine fielder, at home both in the slips, where he was outstanding, and in the deep. Tall, at 6ft 3in, with shoulder-length fair hair, he won a regular place in 1975 when he was awarded his county cap. He had to wait until 1981 and the 223rd innings of his first-class career for his maiden century. It was an heroic effort, withstanding a Sussex attack which included Garth le Roux and Imran Khan for 344 minutes for 101 not out. He came in at number three, but strode to the wicket after Tim Tremlett had been run out off the first ball of the innings without facing. Almost perversely, he recorded his second, and last, century in the very next match when he hit 161 not out at Edgbaston. He was not retained by Hampshire at the end of the following season though the county awarded him a testimonial. He was immensely popular with the Hampshire cricket public and players alike. The latter often looked to him for technical advice. Thereafter, he went to Eton College as a coach to assist another former Hampshire favourite, Vic Cannings. Some 30 years later, John Rice is still working there.

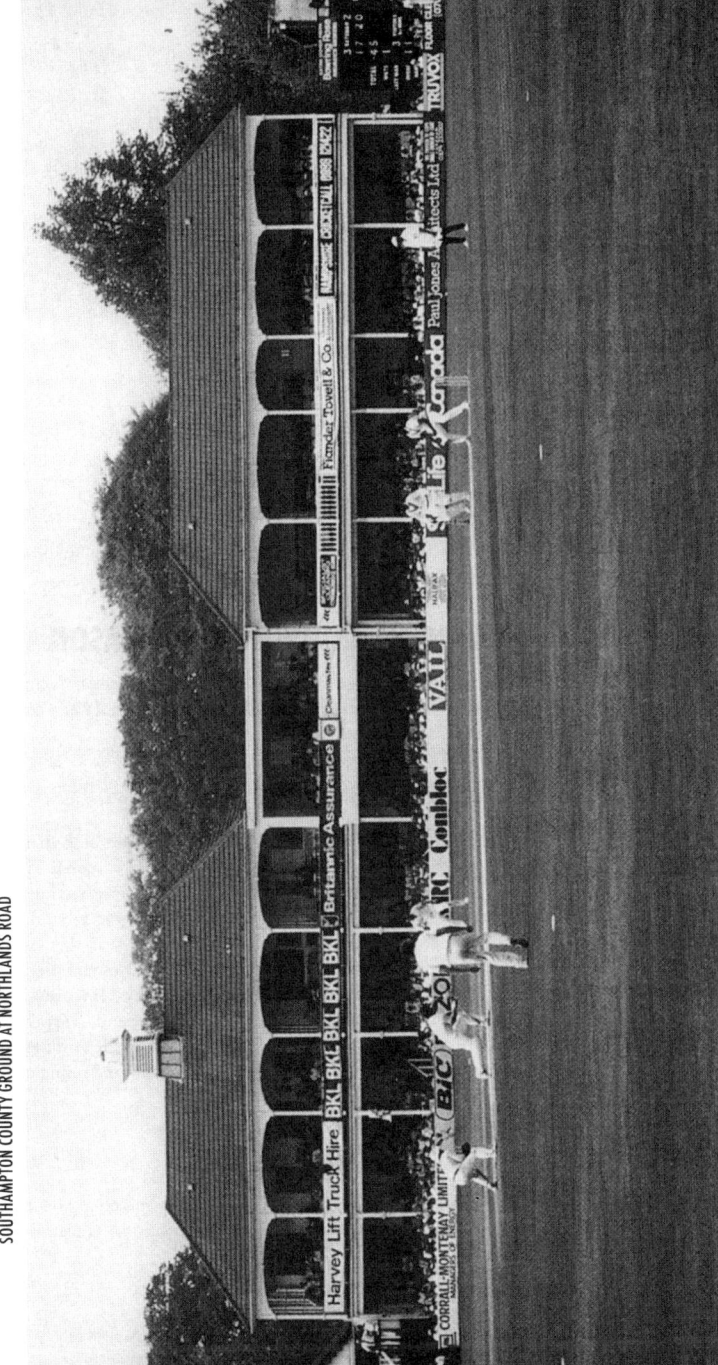

SOUTHAMPTON COUNTY GROUND AT NORTHLANDS ROAD

MOST PROLIFIC ALL-ROUNDERS

Eight men have scored 2,000 runs and taken 150 wickets in List A matches:

Nigel Cowley....................................(2,913 + 233)
Kevan James....................................(2,324 + 223)
Trevor Jesty ....(6,859 + 334)
Malcolm Marshall ....(2,190 + 237)
Dimitri Mascarenhas......................(3,984 + 285)
John Rice..(2,322 + 187)
Peter Sainsbury ....(2,079 + 202)
Shaun Udal.......................................(2,503 + 407)
Sean Ervine......................................(3,233 + 105)

MOST CATCHES IN A MATCH

John Rice is the only man to hold five catches in a match, against Warwickshire at Southampton in the Sunday League in 1978.

MOST PROLIFIC ALL-ROUNDERS IN A SEASON

Three men have scored 300 runs and taken 30 wickets in a season: John Stephenson (386 + 42) in 1997, Shaun Udal (462 + 39) also in 1997 and Dimitri Mascarenhas (334 + 38) in 2000.

WORLD CUP 1975

Gordon Greenidge and Andy Roberts were in the West Indies side that beat Australia in the first World Cup Final in 1975. Greenidge scored 55 in the semi-final against New Zealand at The Oval. Roberts's best bowling analysis was 3-39 against Australia in a group match at the same ground. However, the most memorable performance by either player was that of Roberts with the bat against Pakistan at Edgbaston. After Pakistan totalled 266/7, the West Indies slipped to 203/9. They required 64 off 14 overs. Apart from a potential run-out opportunity nine balls from the end, Deryck Murray and Roberts displayed nerves of steel. Five runs were needed off the final over. Following two leg byes, Roberts picked up two runs and a single to bring the West Indies victory. He was unbeaten on 24.

BARRY RICHARDS ON TV

Bowlers generally became fretful if they knew their match against Hampshire was on television as Barry Richards showed an uncanny tendency to roll out his full artistic repertoire on such occasions. By the time of his departure in 1978, he had scored more runs and centuries in one-day cricket on television than any other player. Perhaps the best of his five televised hundreds was in 1976 when he made 101 out of 127 against leaders Essex at Southampton in the Sunday League. His stroke play brought the crowd to near hysteria. In a display of simply outrageous shot-making he finessed the ball all around the ground, hitting his runs in 71 minutes. He made his second fifty off 21 balls. Just towards the end of his innings, having exhausted his ground strokes, he thought he would go the aerial route and duly deposited two mighty sixes into the top tier of the pavilion to reach his century. He deliberately skied the next one to cover. He was on the way to the pavilion, bat tucked under his arm, by the time the catch was taken.

LOSING SEMI-FINALISTS (3)

With Greenidge and Roberts on tour with the West Indies, and Peter Sainsbury injured for some of the season, Hampshire's form in 1976 was patchy. They did, though, reach the semi-final of the Gillette Cup. Against Northamptonshire at Southampton and before a capacity all-ticket crowd, they made 215/7 in their 60 overs. The only meaningful contributions came from man of the match David Turner (86), Trevor Jesty (37) and a late 28 by Mike Taylor. Northants seemed to be strolling to victory after Roy Virgin (82) and Peter Willey (47) put on 83 for the first wicket. However, with the score at 202/4 with five overs remaining, their nerve began to fail them. John Rice took two wickets, Trevor Jesty bowled a maiden and then claimed another wicket, and Geoff Cook was superbly run out by Turner. Crucially, though, Sarfraz Nawaz had swung Rice for six with 13 balls remaining. With five required off the final over, Sarfraz scored two off the first ball and a single off the third. Bishen Bedi then played and missed but swatted the penultimate ball to the boundary. Hampshire had lost by two wickets.

LOSING SEMI-FINALISTS (4)

Hampshire reached a semi-final for the third consecutive year in 1977. It was in the B & H Cup against Gloucestershire, again before another capacity crowd at Southampton. Gloucestershire started well as Sadiq Mohammad (76) and Andy Stovold (46) put on 106 for the first wicket. However, none of the other batsmen prospered and they were bowled out in the 54th over for 180 (Tom Mottram 3-31 and Mike Taylor 3-37). Hampshire must have fancied their chances but they then ran into a Mike Procter firestorm. He took four wickets in five balls as he dismissed Greenidge, Richards, Rice and Jesty, all bowled leg before wicket. With

Hampshire reeling at 18/4, David Turner and Nigel Cowley set about repairing the ship and did so to great effect as they took the score to 127. Both men, though, were then dismissed in quick succession, the latter by Julian Shackleton by 59. Though there was some stoic late order resistance, Procter (6-13) and Brian Brain accounted for the remaining batsmen. Hampshire finished seven runs short.

SUNDAY CHAMPIONS (2)

John Player (Sunday) League table 1978:

	P	W	L	NR	Pts
Hampshire	16	11	3	2	48
Somerset	16	11	3	2	48
Leicestershire	16	11	3	2	48
Worcestershire	16	10	5	1	42

Hampshire won their second John Player League (JPL) title by virtue of a superior run rate. Of their three JPL successes, it was by far the closest, most controversial and meritorious. With five matches to play during August and September, and Hampshire joint second with Somerset, six points behind and with a game in hand on leaders Worcestershire, Andy Roberts and Barry Richards walked out on the county in the space of four days at the end of July. Up until that stage, Hampshire had won seven of their 11 matches. Two had been abandoned without a ball being bowled, including the first match of the season against Somerset. Paradoxically, Roberts had made major contributions in four of those victories, two of which were with the bat. Richards had opened the campaign with two fifties in winning causes. However, he later moved down the order. It was clear that his enthusiasm was on the wane. The pair, though, had been a major influence in six of the seven successes. However, rather than being despondent about their exits, the team rallied behind captain Richard Gilliat and responded to the situation magnificently. Gilliat assumed responsibility to partner Gordon Greenidge at the top of the order and shared in two century stands and two of over 50. Greenidge took his own game to a new level and reeled off scores of 116 against Yorkshire at Portsmouth, 48 at Cheltenham, 51 against Kent at Southampton and 122 in the final match against Middlesex at Bournemouth. Hampshire won all four of these matches. His only failure resulted in a loss at Northampton. That last match was a thriller. Greenidge was supported in century stands by Gilliat (35) and Jesty (47) as the county posted 221/4. Middlesex were making light work of their reply, until the captain threw the ball to Jesty as the sixth bowler. The latter was always a better first innings bowler but on this occasion he transformed the match with 5-32.

Hampshire won by 26 runs but they and their supporters then had to wait almost half an hour for the result at Taunton. When it was announced that they had lost by one run to Essex, Dean Park erupted. David Turner had sustained the Hampshire batting with five fifties, including 96 and 91 not out in successive wins at Chelmsford and Trent Bridge. Turner (481 runs) and Greenidge (637) led the scorers. Jesty, who also scored 401, took 21 wickets to head the bowling list, though Roberts was top of the averages. John Rice was the leading fielder in the competition with 16 catches, including a record five against Warwickshire at Southampton.

WORLD CUP 1979

Gordon Greenidge and Malcolm Marshall were both members of the West Indies' victorious World Cup squad in 1979, although Marshall did not play. Greenidge was the highest scorer in the competition with 253 runs. He was named man of the match for his 106 not out against India at Edgbaston and again in the semi-final for 73 against Pakistan. Marshall had joined the county at the start of the season.

MATCH TRANSFERRED

In June 1980 Hampshire's Sunday League match against Worcestershire was transferred from Portsmouth to Southampton. The lack of rain in May had not allowed the lumps and bumps to be rolled on the outfield, nor new seed to germinate, after the rugby union season.

JEFF THOMSON

Australian fast bowler Jeff Thomson took 7-22 for Middlesex against Hampshire at Lord's in a B & H group match in 1981. His figures remain the best by a bowler against Hampshire in a List A match. Notwithstanding his efforts Hampshire prevailed by one wicket. The match finished at 8.25pm.

BARREN B & H RUN

The above match was Hampshire's first B & H tie of the 1981 season. They then endured a sequence of seven losses and one no result in the competition. They did not win another match until May 1983, when they beat holders Somerset in a low-scoring encounter at Taunton.

HAMPSHIRE'S FIRST ENGLAND REPRESENTATIVE

Trevor Jesty became the first Hampshire man to represent England in ODIs when he played against Australia in January 1983. Hampshire supporters thought his selection was overdue. He had been flown out as a replacement for Derek Randall in the one-day series. In the event, Randall was fit to participate but Jesty played on merit. He played in ten ODIs in the next month, his sole appearances on the international stage. His best score was 52 not out off only 34 balls against New Zealand at Adelaide. He reached his fifty by hitting the last ball of the innings into the pavilion.

UNUSUAL DISMISSAL PROMPTS COLLAPSE

In the B & H quarter-final against Kent at Canterbury in 1983, David Turner was caught and bowled after the ball rebounded off non-striker Paul Terry's body. His dismissal prompted a collapse, the last six wickets falling for 24 runs as Hampshire finished five runs short.

LOSING SEMI-FINALISTS (5)

After Hampshire lost their Sunday League match and the above encounter to Kent, the latter then disposed of them in the semi-finals of the NatWest Trophy by 71 runs. All three matches were played at Canterbury. Malcolm Marshall took 4-15 as Kent were dismissed for 173 (Chris Tavare 64). Hampshire's response was a disaster. Of the top order batsmen, only Chris Smith (25) and Mark Nicholas (25) made double figures. They were bowled out for just 102. Only a last-wicket stand of eight avoided Hampshire being dismissed for their lowest total in Gillette/NatWest matches at the time. Man of the match was Kent's Eldine Baptiste who had figures of 5-20.

HAMPSHIRE HOST FIRST INTERNATIONAL

In 1983, Hampshire hosted their first ODI when Australia played Zimbabwe at Southampton in the World Cup. The former won a fascinating duel by 32 runs. Zimbabwe had defeated Australia at Trent Bridge earlier in the competition. On this occasion, with eight overs remaining, Zimbabwe required 61 with five wickets in hand. Rodney Hogg (3-40) and Trevor Chappell (3-47) ensured that history would not be repeated.

WORLD CUP 1983

Gordon Greenidge and Malcolm Marshall were in the West Indies side that suffered a shock defeat to India in the World Cup Final at Lord's.

Prior to the final, Greenidge was named man of the match when he made 105 not out against Zimbabwe at Worcester. He also scored 90 against Australia at Lord's. Marshall finished second behind New Zealand's Richard Hadlee in the event's bowling averages (12 wickets at 14.58). Trevor Jesty was in the England squad but did not play.

GREENIDGE AND JESTY AT PORTSMOUTH

There have been few, if any, more diverting partnerships as that between Gordon Greenidge and Trevor Jesty in the Sunday League against Surrey at Portsmouth in 1983. After Chris Smith had been dismissed at 23, the pair added an unbroken 269. It was a stand of contrasts. Greenidge, as normal, put body and soul into every shot but never quite found his timing. On the other hand, Jesty's touch was sublime as he bisected the field at will, as if by radar. Greenidge made 108 not out (one six and nine fours) and Jesty 166 not out (three sixes and 18 fours). Jesty's innings was the highest of his career in List A matches and remained a record at Portsmouth.

TREVOR JESTY

Trevor Jesty would figure prominently in debate on the best Hampshire-born cricketer to play for the county. For those who saw him play, his attractive stroke play and valuable right-arm medium pace swing bowling will live long in the memory. Besides his exploits mentioned in the previous pages, he was a major force in first-class cricket. It was worth the price of admission just to see his walk to the wicket. It was brisk and confident, reminiscent of a yacht under full sail in the Solent. Gosport-born, of medium height and blond haired, his handsome strokes matched his countenance. His glory was the cover drive which was so reminiscent of the princely Barry Richards that it was often difficult to tell them apart. Jesty first played for Hampshire in 1966 as an emergency opening bowler. He became a regular in 1969 and was awarded his cap in 1971.

As a batsman, his class was always apparent – he just oozed it – but he was unable to translate that talent into making centuries until 1976. His first was predictably glorious, 134 against Gloucestershire, when he and Richard Gilliat added 237 in only 140 minutes. A few weeks later, he rescued Hampshire after Ian Botham had taken six wickets for one run, by scoring an unbeaten 159 out of a total of 296. He also returned his career best bowling figures of 7-75 against Worcestershire at Southampton in that year. His great year was in 1982. Enjoying a well-earned benefit, he posted a career best aggregate and average (1,645 runs at 58.75). He also scored eight centuries, the most by any Hampshire player since Phil Mead in 1933. During an innings of 133 against Pakistan at Bournemouth, he hit the leg-spin wizard Abdul Qadir for 26 in one over, and ended the season by scoring a century in 64 minutes against Warwickshire at Southampton. *Wisden* nominated him as one of its Five Cricketers of the Year but he was not selected for the ensuing winter tour of Australia. His omission caused a furore, consuming many column inches. The fact that he was subsequently flown out as a replacement for the one-day series was regarded as an act of contrition by the selectors. Though he was in England's World Cup squad in 1983, he never played a Test. His talent was recognised in 2010 when, with Peter Sainsbury, he was one of the selections by a panel of experts in *Wisden Cricket Monthly* for the best post-war England team of players who never won a cap. Unfortunately, Jesty left Hampshire in acrimonious circumstances at the end of the 1984 season after he had been passed over for the captaincy. He went on to enjoy seven more seasons in county cricket with Surrey and Lancashire. He became a first-class umpire in 1994 and has officiated as a reserve umpire in Tests and one-day internationals, and women's Tests.

CHRIS SMITH IN ODIS

Chris Smith played for England in four ODIs on the tour of New Zealand and Pakistan in 1983/84. His best score was 70 against the former at Wellington. In his sole ODI in Pakistan, he became the first Hampshire player to take a wicket in such matches. His looping off-breaks produced 2-8 at Karachi.

YOUNGEST MAN OF THE MATCH

Eighteen-year-old Stephen Andrew made a remarkable debut for Hampshire in the B & H match with Surrey at The Oval in 1984. The tall right-arm fast-medium bowler took 3-12 for which he won the man of the match award, the youngest player to do so. Andrew went on to play in Hampshire's first Lord's final success in 1988. Unfortunately, he suffered a number of injuries. He rejected the offer of a new contract at the end of the following season and joined Essex, for whom he played until 1992.

YOUNGEST CENTURY-MAKER

In August 1984, Robin Smith became the youngest Hampshire player to score a century in List A matches when he blitzed 104 against Glamorgan at Sophia Gardens, Cardiff. He was 20 years 335 days old. He reached his century off 82 balls, sharing a fourth-wicket stand of 115 with his brother Chris (29) along the way. He went on to score a measured 51 in the next match against Essex at Colchester. It was clear that a special talent had arrived on the scene.

LOSING SEMI-FINALISTS (6)

After comprehensively disposing of Berkshire, Leicestershire and Somerset en route to the semi-final of the NatWest Trophy in 1985, Hampshire supporters were optimistic that this would be their year to reach Lord's for the first time. Their hopes were dashed by the toss and a controversial umpiring decision. Their opponents, Essex, won the toss and asked Hampshire to bat on a damp pitch conducive to seam bowling. They duly struggled to 224/8. Though six batsmen passed 20, Mark Nicholas's 39 was the highest innings. By now the pitch had eased. Essex had reached 125/3 when Graham Gooch, on 53, was given the benefit of the doubt as Robin Smith's direct throw hit the stumps at the umpire's end. A photograph was to show that the England opener was well short of his ground. After bad light stopped play, and the match resumed next morning, Gooch went on to score 93 not out to take his side to 224/7. Essex thus reached the final by virtue of losing fewer wickets.

SUNDAY CHAMPIONS (3)

John Player Special (Sunday) League table 1986:

................................P	W	L	NR	Pts
Hampshire 16	12	3	1	50
Essex 16	11	4	1	46
Nottinghamshire......16	10	5	1	42
Sussex......................16	10	6	–	40
Northamptonshire ...16	9	5	2	40

Given their unequivocal support to the original concept of limited-overs league cricket, it was particularly fitting that Hampshire should gain the title in the last year of John Player's 18-year sponsorship. Hampshire won eight of their first nine matches. However, they then suffered a frustrating three-week period as the match at Cheltenham was abandoned, and defeats were suffered at the hands of Sussex and Middlesex. A Gordon Greenidge blitz (125 not out) against Yorkshire at Bournemouth returned them to the top of the table and inspired batting by Greenidge again (51) and the Smith brothers (Robin 95; Chris 73) formed the foundation of a 73-run win against Derbyshire at Heanor. The county therefore travelled to The Oval for the penultimate match requiring victory to secure the league title. Their supporters were in danger of cardiac arrest as the game swung dramatically throughout. On an awkward pitch Hampshire, despite 51 from Gordon Greenidge, were 95/7 at one stage. Kevan James then hit a maiden half-century in the competition and, with Bob Parks, added a crucial 35 in the final five overs. Hampshire's total of 149/8 looked quite healthy as Surrey subsided to 117/6. With 29 required off 16 balls, David Thomas (33) then hit a six and four, and was dropped by Cardigan Connor off a skier. Seven runs were eventually required off the last over to be bowled by Connor. Thomas was unable to score off his first two balls and was well caught by James off the third. Andy Needham was then run out by the ubiquitous James as he attempted a second run. Tony Gray therefore needed a six to win the match for Surrey, or four to tie off the last ball. It yielded only a single. Connor had conceded only two runs off the over and Hampshire had won by three. Their victory in the final match against Lancashire at Southampton was a coronation affair. Robin Smith (629 runs), Greenidge (493) and Paul Terry (472) scored the most runs. Six bowlers took ten wickets or more, the most productive being Tim Tremlett (26).

CARDIGAN CONNOR

The Anguilla-born Cardigan Adolphous Connor went on to become one of the most dangerous new-ball bowlers in county cricket. When he perfected the leg-cutter in the early 1990s, and the white ball was added to the mix shortly afterwards, top-order batsmen received the sternest of examinations. His heart, stamina and accuracy were a byword. He was blessed with a natural athlete's grace. He simply flowed over the ground in his run-up. Connor had the build of a middleweight boxer. Even in his mid-30s his frame carried no spare flesh, testament to his pride in his profession and the high standards which he set himself. He never gave anything less than his best even when not fully fit. He was one of the most courageous of cricketers; his damaged knees were as famous as Denis Compton's in another era. Connor also possessed the readiest of smiles. All these traits endeared him to Hampshire followers for well over a decade. He originally came to England at the age of 15 to join his family. He then spent the following seven summers playing club cricket in the Thames Valley area and for Buckinghamshire in the Minor Counties Championship. A right-arm fast-medium bowler, of medium height and invariably shaven headed, Connor made his debut for Hampshire in 1984. He gave instant notice of his ability by taking 3-15 in his opening ten-over spell. He was capped in 1988. Besides the Sunday League triumph on the previous page, Connor played in Hampshire's victorious sides in their first three Lord's cup finals between 1988 and 1992. His three most memorable performances were all in his final years with Hampshire. In first-class cricket there was his lionhearted 7-47 against Northamptonshire in 1994, and his record 9-38 against Gloucestershire two years later, the best ever figures of any bowler at Southampton. In his penultimate season he predicted how he would dismiss each Essex batsman in the NatWest Trophy second round tie. In an amazing first over he duly took wickets with his first, third and sixth balls and added another soon after. Connor's aggressive batting was always crowd pleasing.

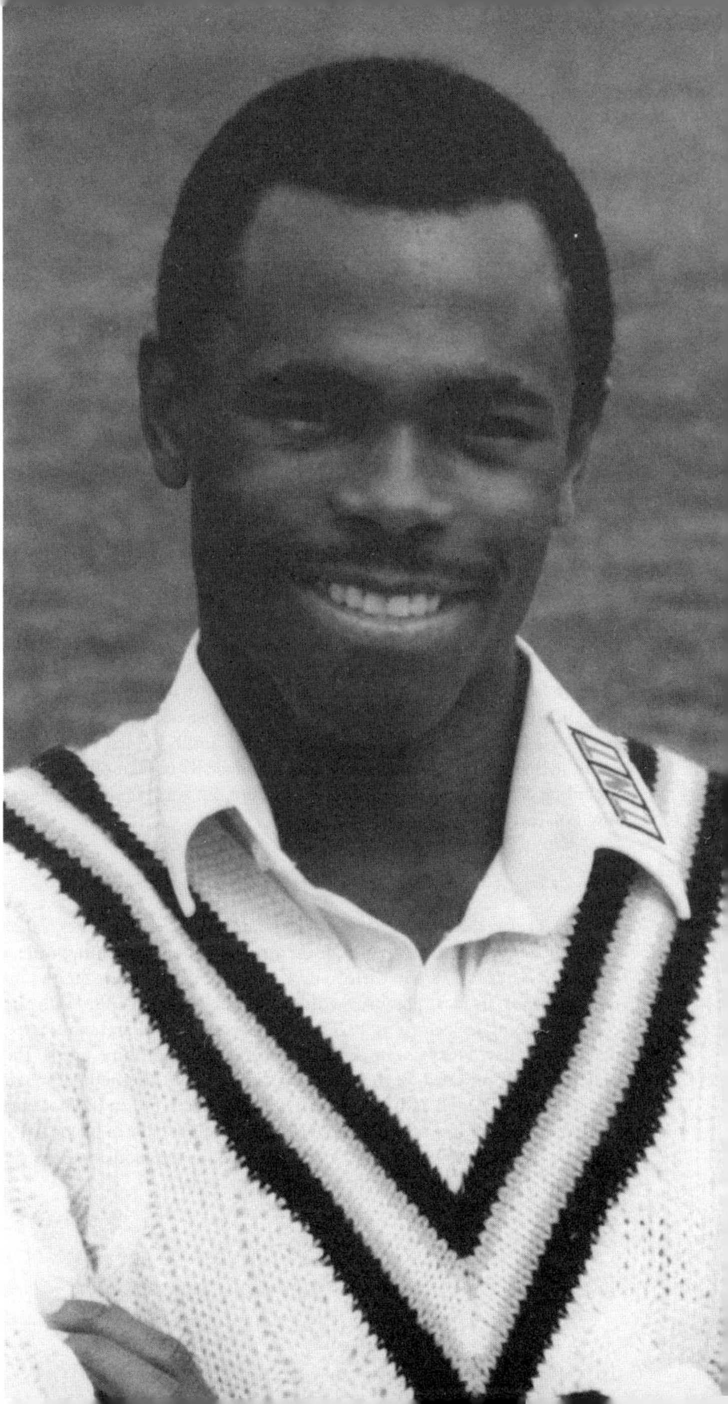

CARDIGAN CONNOR

He was a very clean hitter of the ball and it is surprising he scored only two first-class fifties, the highest of which was 59 against Surrey at The Oval in 1993 when he was sent in as a night watchman. After retiring in 1999 with 1,021 wickets in all competitions, Connor returned to his native island. He is now involved in coaching there.

LAST BALL THRILLERS

Four Sunday League matches were decided off the last ball in 1987. Two consecutive matches at Southampton, against Gloucestershire and Derbyshire, finished in a tie. In the other two games Hampshire won at Leicester by five runs but lost to Sussex at Horsham by one wicket.

ROBIN SMITH HEROICS

Even by Robin Smith's standards, his innings against Worcestershire in the quarter-finals at New Road in 1988 deserved to be accorded heroic status. In a match played over three days because of rain, and on a wicket that became increasingly spiteful, Worcestershire totalled 169, which they owed chiefly to bold hitting by Martin Weston (50). All four of Hampshire's pace bowlers, headed by South African Steve Jefferies (4-34), shared the wickets. When Hampshire batted they seemed destined to lose when the seventh wicket fell at 114. However, Smith was still there and he was joined by Nigel Cowley. Hampshire never lost another wicket as the streetwise Cowley bravely kept him company. Smith guided Hampshire over the line with 11 balls to spare. He had made 87 not out off 141 balls, including 11 fours and a five. Cowley's 18 not out was Hampshire's next highest score.

LORD'S AT LAST

A fortnight after the match at Worcester, Hampshire travelled to Chelmsford to play Essex in the semi-final. On the first day, the Hampshire bowlers contained Essex to 238/6 in their 55 overs. Paul Terry and Chris Smith (56) then provided an ideal platform with an opening stand of 118. With the county strolling to victory, at 192/1 off 46 overs, rain fell and terminated play for the day. Forty-seven runs were still required off nine overs. The match was not resumed on the following day until late afternoon. Though David Turner (31) fell early on, Terry (109) and Robin Smith (20 not out) steered the county to a seven-wicket victory with eight balls in hand. After 25 years of limited overs cricket, and heartbreak in the semi-finals on six occasions, Hampshire had reached a Lord's final at last.

LORD'S FINALS (1)

Benson & Hedges Cup – 9 July 1988
Derbyshire 117 (Steve Jefferies 5-13);
Hampshire 118/3 (Robin Smith 38)
Hampshire won by seven wickets
Man of the match: Steve Jefferies

Hampshire were in complete control of the match from the start. Mark Nicholas won the toss and, in ideal conditions for swing bowling, chose to bowl first. The South African Steve Jefferies exploited the conditions magnificently. He bowled Kim Barnett for 13 whereupon Nicholas decided to post himself under the helmet at short leg. It was a captaincy master-stroke which brought immediate success. Peter Bowler edged Jefferies to Nicholas the very next ball and there was a reprise shortly afterwards which accounted for Bruce Roberts. When Jefferies trapped Goldsmith leg before, Derbyshire were 32/4. Jefferies went on to take 5-13 in ten overs – the best analysis at the time in a Lord's final. It was small wonder that he won the gold award as the man of the match. Apart from John Morris (42) no batsman could break the stranglehold imposed by the Hampshire bowlers. Nigel Cowley conceded only 17 runs and took one wicket in his 11 overs. Cardigan Connor (2-27) hit the stumps in successive balls to account for the last two wickets. Derbyshire had been dismissed for 117 in 46.3 overs. In their turn, Hampshire were 44/2 early on. The wickets were those of the openers, Paul Terry and Chris Smith, who were instrumental in Hampshire's semi-final win at Chelmsford. However, Robin Smith then played a thunderous cameo of 38 in 27 balls to prise the door wide open for Hampshire. He simply launched into the Derbyshire fast bowlers with a succession of rousing boundaries. He eventually fell to a marvellous boundary catch by Goldsmith behind the wicketkeeper off a top-edged hook. Smith had, though, demonstrated that he was a big-match player. He won his first England cap within weeks. Nicholas (35 not out) and, appropriately, David Turner, in his 23rd season, saw Hampshire home in 31.5 overs. The end was an anti-climax; the winning run coming off a no ball. The Hampshire supporters swarmed onto the field to acclaim their heroes. After waiting for so long for Lord's success, the roar which greeted Nicholas gleefully holding the cup aloft was befitting of the occasion.

DAVID TURNER

David Turner had become the first Hampshire player to play in five title-winning sides, having appeared in the championship-winning team of 1973, the three Sunday League successes and a Lord's cup victory. The Wiltshire-born diminutive left-handed batsman had figured in five of the six semi-final defeats so the Lord's win must have been a very sweet moment indeed. He made his Hampshire debut as a 17-year-old in 1966 and remained an indispensable part of the scene until his retirement in 1989. Supporters will remember with considerable affection the man with the low back-lift and the streetwise technique. They will recall the dab down to third man, his ferocious pulling and cutting of anything short and the power of his driving stemming from his strong forearms. His most famous innings was a scintillating 131 against the Australians in 1972. This innings was to lead to him being touted as an England player but, shortly afterwards, he pulled a ball into his face at Basingstoke and was never quite the same batsman again. Turner's batting, though, matured with age. His average over the last seven years of his career was 50 per cent better than in his first 17. He scored 28,425 runs in all cricket for Hampshire – an aggregate exceeded only by four batsmen in the county's history. His fielding also caught the imagination. His speed over the ground and the awesome power of his throw, made him one of the most respected fieldsmen of his era. Even when approaching 40 Turner still patrolled far greater areas of the outfield than his younger colleagues. Given the reduction in the one day programme, his 377 appearances in List A matches may well stand the test of time. He also made 416 appearances in first-class cricket; similarly, it is possible that he may be the last Hampshire player to play more than 400 times in such cricket for the county. After his retirement, he returned to the family shoe business in his native Chippenham.

ROBIN SMITH IN ODIS

Robin Smith made his debut in ODI for England against Sri Lanka at The Oval in September 1988. He went on to play in 71 ODIs until 1996, scoring 2,419 runs (average 39.01). Among his four centuries was England's highest score in ODIs, 167 not out against Australia at Edgbaston in 1993.

MOST CATCHES IN A SEASON

Robin Smith held 20 catches in 1988, the most by a fielder in a season in List A matches for Hampshire.

BEATEN SEMI-FINALISTS (7)

After winning the Benson & Hedges Cup in 1988, Hampshire came tantalisingly close to reaching Lord's again in that season, and in each of the next two summers. On all three occasions the matches were in the NatWest Trophy. The last two were played at Southampton. They lost to

BENSON & HEDGES CUP 1988-THE SIDE AFTER THEIR SEMI-FINAL VICTORY

Worcestershire at New Road by 21 runs in 1988, to Middlesex by three runs a year later and then to Northamptonshire by one run in 1990. At this stage, therefore, Hampshire had played five semi-finals at Northlands Road and lost them all. It seemed, indeed, a hoodoo ground.

DAVID GOWER IN ODIS

David Gower played the last nine of his 114 appearances for England in ODIs while with Hampshire. His highest score in those matches in 1990 and 1991 was 50 against India at Headingley.

THOUSAND RUNS IN A SEASON

In 1991, Chris Smith became the first, and so far, only Hampshire batsman to score 1,000 runs in List A matches in a season. His tally was 1,004 (average 77.23). He left the county after the NatWest Trophy semi-final win against Warwickshire. If he had delayed his departure until the end of the season, he could have played in another three fixtures and would almost certainly have added to his aggregate. Smith had begun the season with a gluttonous feast of run scoring: 86 v Yorkshire in the Sunday League, and then 121 v Nottinghamshire, 78 not out v Minor Counties at Trowbridge and 142 v Glamorgan, all in the B & H Cup. The matches against the counties were all at Southampton.

MOST CENTURIES IN A SEASON

Chris Smith scored four centuries in List A matches in 1991, a Hampshire record at the time. It was to be equalled by his brother Robin in 1993.

LORD'S FINAL (2) – THE PRELUDE

In 1992, Hampshire moved almost seamlessly through to the final of the NatWest Trophy after comprehensive wins against Berkshire, Lancashire, Nottinghamshire and Warwickshire at Edgbaston in the semi-final. However, in the three weeks before the final, Hampshire were dealt two hammer blows. The first came two days after Edgbaston when it was confirmed that Chris Smith would not be available for the final as he was contracted to take up a marketing post with the Western Australian Cricket Association in Perth. It transpired he had originally signed in June to take up his appointment at the beginning of August. At that time he felt Hampshire had as much chance of reaching Lord's as 'flying to the Moon'. He was subsequently granted a three-week reprieve due to the birth of his daughter. The second bombshell exploded on the Thursday before the final when Mark Nicholas's hand was terminally damaged for the season by Waqar Younis. By one of those coincidences, Hampshire were required to play Surrey in a four-day championship match immediately before the final. On a fast track at The Oval, Waqar created havoc, taking 12 wickets and bowling Surrey to an uncomfortably one-sided victory in the process. Tony Middleton, who had never previously played in a NatWest Trophy match, replaced Smith, David Gower captained in lieu of Nicholas, and Jon Ayling was drafted into the side. All three were to prove inspired choices.

LORD'S FINAL (2) – THE MATCH

NatWest Trophy – 7 September 1991
Surrey 240/5 in 60 overs (Alec Stewart 61, Graham Thorpe 93; Cardigan Connor 3-39);
Hampshire 243/6 in 59.4 overs (Tony Middleton 78, Robin Smith 78)
Hampshire won by four wickets
Man of the match: Robin Smith

After winning the toss and electing to field on a sunny and warm day, Hampshire's bowlers restricted Surrey to 240/5 on a good pitch. Though Stewart and Thorpe added 114 for the second wicket, and David Ward made a rapid 43, their batting never achieved any damaging command. Hampshire's cause was assisted greatly by Cardigan Connor's three wickets in his final spell towards the end of the innings. Paul Terry and Tony Middleton responded wonderfully well. By punishing the loose ball and shrewd running between the wickets, they had put on 85 in 25 overs by tea.

Terry was run out in the second over after the resumption, but Robin Smith ensured that Surrey were unable to capitalise. The pair added 70 before Middleton (78) was yorked by Tony Murphy. It had been a wonderfully composed innings. Two more wickets, those of David Gower and Kevan James, then fell in quick succession. Jon Ayling then joined Smith. Hampshire were now 193/4; 48 runs to win with eight overs remaining. The situation remained tense as, like the Surrey batsmen before them, the pair were never able to dominate. With four overs to go Hampshire still needed 34. Despite Smith's presence, the situation was becoming decidedly tense. The light was now also extremely murky. The lights in the Tavern area were shining with lighthouse-like intensity. When Ayling upper-cut Murphy into the Tavern for six and on-drove the next ball for four, it seemed as if Hampshire would win comfortably. But at the end of the same over, Smith's drive ricocheted from the stumps at the bowler's end to Murphy, who threw down the wicket before Smith (78) was able to recover his ground. Hampshire eventually needed four off the last over. In near darkness, Adi Aymes, slipping on the now dewy surface in answering Ayling's call, was run out as the bowler, Martin Bicknell, effected another direct hit. Rajesh Maru squirted his first ball off an inside edge to short fine leg for a single. Ayling glanced the next through backward square leg for four, and victory. The Hampshire team had overcome considerable adversity to become the worthiest of winners.

JON AYLING

Portsmouth-born Jon Ayling went on to play in all three of Hampshire's first cup-winning sides at Lord's. However, his career was cruelly cut short by a crippling knee injury at the age of 25. He originally sustained the injury in a pre-season friendly in 1989 in an accidental collision with Sussex's David Smith. He missed that season and played on stoically until 1992, but at the start of the next season, he decided he could no longer continue. His retirement coincided with the start of a bleak period for the county. The former Portsmouth Grammar School pupil was the first Hampshire-born player to cement his place in the county side since Trevor Jesty 20 years earlier.

He played in the 1988 B & H final just two months after his first-class debut. His accurate pace bowling, allied to the disconcerting bounce generated by his height, were important factors in all three cup runs. As, of course, was his batting against Surrey (see previous page). After his first season in the game he was talked about in some quarters as a successor to Ian Botham. He was undoubtedly a genuine all-rounder. Ayling's forte as a batsman was his front-foot driving. He hit the ball colossal distances when his eye was in; as far as more notable strikers of sixes such as Gordon Greenidge and Robin Smith. His first nine scoring shots in first-class cricket, against Oxford University in The Parks, were all boundaries (eight fours and a six). The first weekend after his retirement he struck 11 sixes as he savaged the Andover bowlers in the Southern League. Before the injury Ayling could make good batsmen hurry on fairly benign wickets. At the time he was the only Hampshire bowler ever to take a wicket with his first ball in first-class cricket. With the knee injury he lost some of his zip but compensated by developing varieties. His capabilities are demonstrated by his finishing third in the first-class averages in 1992. His fielding, particularly in one-saving positions, was intimidating to the batsman. After the injury he lost some pace over the ground but still caught most capably. Ayling rejoined Hampshire as a bowling coach in 2008 and is now cricket professional at Dauntsey's School in Wiltshire.

SUNDAY LEAGUE TRAVAILS

Hampshire finished at the foot of the Sunday League for the first time in 1991. They won two of their first three matches and the last, but in between they went 12 games without a win: 11 losses and one no result. The sequence included seven consecutive losses, a record for the county in List A matches. They also gained only 14 points, another record low. Hampshire endured a torrid time in the Sunday League for much of the decade. After obtaining third place in the following season, they never finished higher than 12th until 1998. They finished at the foot of the table again in 1995. In 1998, they rose to eighth, which enabled them to qualify for Division One in the two-divisional structure in 1999.

A DAVID GOWER CLASSIC

David Gower scored his only century for Hampshire in List A matches early in the 1992 B & H Cup run in a group match against Northamptonshire at Southampton. After rain had washed out the first day, and part of the second, the match was reduced to 33 overs a side on a pitch at the edge of the square. With a short boundary on that side of the ground, Gower stroked 118 not out off 95 balls (three sixes and seven fours), despite the attentions of West Indian fast bowler Curtly Ambrose. In reply to Hampshire's 197/6, the visitors eventually needed seven off the last two balls with five wickets still in hand. However, Rob Bailey (109 not out) was unable to make contact off either ball bowled by Cardigan Connor.

FREEZING IN GLASGOW

In 1992 Hampshire played Scotland for the first time in the B & H Cup at Glasgow. They were greeted by freezing and considerably wet conditions. Scotland's Barbadian professional, George Reifer, wore six sweaters during his innings of 63 not out. Scotland totalled 151/5. Hampshire were in trouble at 16/2, having lost Tony Middleton and David Gower (first ball), before rain brought play to a close on the first day. Overnight heavy rain then prevented any play on the second. The match was therefore designated a no result.

BOGEY BEATEN

Hampshire laid their Northlands Road semi-final hoodoo when they defeated Somerset by six wickets in the B & H semi-final in the above year. After Somerset posted 218/8 (Cardigan Connor 3-32), Hampshire reached their target with 11 balls to spare. Man of the match Paul Terry finished with an unbeaten 89.

FIFTY WICKETS IN A SEASON

In 1992, Shaun Udal became the first, and so far only, bowler to take 50 wickets in a season in List A matches. He claimed 51 victims. The next most prolific bowlers have been Cardigan Connor (43 in 1991 and 40 in 1989), John Stephenson (42 in 1997) and Stephen Jefferies (41 in 1998).

LORD'S FINAL (3)

Benson and Hedges Cup – 11 and 12 July 1992
Hampshire 253/5 in 55 overs (Robin Smith 90);
Kent 212 in 52.3 overs (Mark Benson 59; Malcolm Marshall 3-33;
Shaun Udal 3-67)
Hampshire won by 41 runs
Man of the match: Robin Smith

The weather on the first day was more fit for football. Hampshire were asked to bat first on a seam bowler's paradise. However, Paul Terry (41) and Tony Middleton (27) scored off every opportunity, disrupting the field with cheeky singles, to see Hampshire off to a positive start as they added 68 off 19 overs. A world-class third wicket partnership of 85 between David Gower (29) and Robin Smith (90) helped pushed the score along at six an over. Smith was calculating throughout, one six being despatched to the top deck of the Edrich Stand. Mark Nicholas (25) and Malcolm Marshall (29 not out) both scored at better than a run a ball at the end. Given the conditions, poor light, drizzle, interruptions and delays, Hampshire's total of 253/5 was of miraculous dimensions. Play was abandoned for the day after Kent faced just two overs. The quality of Hampshire's batting was demonstrated next morning. On a bright, sunny morning – the two days could not have been more contrasting – the Kent batsmen never came to terms with the movement off the pitch gained by the Hampshire bowlers for the first hour and a half. The irrepressible Marshall (3-33), aided by Cardigan Connor, Jon Ayling, Kevan James and Shaun Udal, all frustrated the Kent batsmen. The wickets of Mark Benson (59) and Carl Hooper (28) in successive overs, the latter to Udal's faster ball, were killer blows. The fielders also played their part. Though the ground fielding looked ragged on occasions, the quality of the catching offered compensations. Bob Parks and Gower took two each; the latter's second – fielding at slip – to dismiss Davies off Marshall was a collector's piece. Most memorably of all, Nicholas took a sensational catch high to his left at wide mid-off, to interrupt an Exocet launched by the dangerous Matthew Fleming (32). The presentations were as emotional as ever, none more so than when the captain asked Marshall to hold the cup aloft. After some initial reservations, the sheer joy of the Bajan's response was a sight to behold.

SHAUN UDAL IN ODIS

When he was a television pundit, Ray Illingworth was full of praise for Shaun Udal's off-spin bowling. It was no surprise, therefore, that when Illingworth became chairman of selectors, he fast-tracked Udal into the international side. Udal made his England ODI debut in 1994 against New Zealand. He played a total of ten ODIs in 1994 and 1995. Almost unbelievably, he was recalled to the national colours over ten years later for his 11th and final appearance, against Pakistan at Rawalpindi. In all matches, he took nine wickets (average 44.44) at the creditable economy rate of 3.92.

LOSING SEMI-FINALISTS (8)

Hampshire reached a semi-final for the sixth time in seven years in 1994. Their opponents were Worcestershire at New Road. Hampshire struggled initially but thanks to Robin Smith (108) they accrued 244/6. Worcestershire were also slow early on and lost two wickets for 22. Graeme Hick and Tom Moody then added 74 before the former was run out. By now, the light was poor and there was rain about. Play was abandoned for the day with the odds slightly in favour of Hampshire. However, Worcester regrouped next morning and Moody (56), Gavin Haynes (63) and David Leatherdale (30) brought them home with 14 balls to spare. Play had been delayed for a while on the first morning when an ambulance came on to the field to allow a spectator to receive emergency life-saving treatment on the outfield. Thankfully, the person later recovered.

B & H DOLDRUMS

The semi-final at Worcester was the last highlight of Hampshire's B & H fortunes. In the next nine years until the competition's cessation in 2002 they reached the quarter-finals only once, in 2000, and were defeated by Glamorgan in Cardiff. In the period from 1995–2002 Hampshire played 35 matches, winning only nine and losing 21. There were five no results. Only six of their victories were against county sides. The other three were against Ireland and British Universities (twice).

MOST CATCHES IN CAREER

Paul Terry held 145 catches, the most by a fielder in List A matches for Hampshire.

IRELAND

Hampshire played Ireland in a List A match at Southampton for the first time in the B & H Cup in 1996. The county's 268/5 included an unbeaten partnership of 100 in only 9.2 overs, between John Stephenson (124 not out) and Winston Benjamin (58 not out). The shell-shocked Irish were then bowled out for 102. They first played in Dublin for a C & G tie in 2006, winning by eight wickets. Hampshire were also due to meet Ireland in a Friends Provident Trophy match in 2009 at Eglinton, near Londonderry, but play was abandoned without a ball being bowled.

ROBIN SMITH'S LAST EPIC

Robin Smith played his last great epic innings in List A matches in a NatWest match at Worcester in 1996. Coming to the middle after the first wicket had fallen at 34, he was hesitant at first and it was his junior partner, Jason Laney (82), who showed the way. However, as he settled and began to find his touch, there was no stopping him. He blazed his way to 158 off 151 balls (two sixes and 21 fours), his highest score for Hampshire in one-day cricket. He and Laney added 179 for the second wicket as Hampshire rushed to 328/6. In reply, Worcestershire were undone by Kevan James, who took three wickets in consecutive overs, including the dangerous Graeme Hick, and Cardigan Connor, who dismissed Vikram Solanki and Tom Moody in the same over. Hampshire won by 125 runs.

NATWEST TROPHY TROUBLES

The above match at Worcester was Hampshire's first victory against a county in the competition since their final success in 1991. In the intervening years from 1996 until the end of the knock-out competition (later sponsored by C & G) in 2005, Hampshire continued to struggle as they had done in the other two one-day tournaments. Though able to defeat non first-class sides, they crashed out to counties at the first time of asking on six further occasions. They did, however, reach the semi-final in 1998 (lost to Lancashire at Southampton by one wicket) and 2000 (defeated by Warwickshire at Edgbaston by 19 runs). In 2005, they won the final.

JOHN STEPHENSON

Hampshire's captain at the start of their decline in the one-day competitions during the 1990s was John Stephenson. He joined Hampshire from Essex in 1995 and assumed the captaincy after the retirement of Mark Nicholas in 1996. It was a difficult remit as he inherited a side in transition, and one that was beset by injuries. However, he never gave less than his best, frequently putting himself at the vanguard with both bat and ball in all competitions. He was an adaptable right-handed batsman, able to play the game most suited to his side's needs. Perhaps his most thrilling innings in one-day cricket was against Lancashire at Southampton in the National League in 1999. When Muttiah Muralitharan came on to bowl, Stephenson smacked his first three balls for two sixes and a four. He eventually made 96 (five sixes and eight fours). He made seven centuries for Hampshire, three of which were in List A matches. In all matches for Hampshire, he scored 6,320 runs and took 316 wickets. Stephenson was a combative cricketer. His approach was an important legacy in the county's history as, above all, he helped them come to terms with the requirements of four-day cricket. Robin Smith replaced him as captain in 1998 but he continued to play for Hampshire until 2001. He then returned to Essex. He is now MCC's head of cricket.

DUCKWORTH-LEWIS

Hampshire first experienced the Duckworth-Lewis method of scoring in their AXA Life (Sunday) League match at Derby in 1997. Hampshire totalled 170/7 in 33 overs. Due to the complexities of the method, Derbyshire were actually required to score more runs than Hampshire. They reached 182/6 in 32.1 overs, thereby winning the match.

FIRST FLOODLIT MATCH

Hampshire played their first match under lights against Warwickshire at Edgbaston in 1999. After Warwickshire had been dismissed for 128, Hampshire were reduced to 114/9. However, Giles White (32 not out) and last man Cardigan Connor (seven not out) enabled Hampshire to scrape home by one wicket in a nail-biting finish. In a match which was televised, White had survived a particularly anxious moment in a narrow stumping decision by the third umpire.

TWO DIVISIONS, MARKETING AND MASCOTS

The Sunday League was replaced by a National League, divided into two divisions, in 1999. The matches were played over 45 overs, rather than 40. Sky television coverage also meant that games could be played on any day of the week. The league heralded a new commercial era as teams played under new nomenclatures in the competition with the associated potential income accruing from the sale of coloured clothing. Hampshire were rebadged Hampshire Hawks. Their mascot, Harry the Hawk, was first spotted at Grace Road, Leicester, in the first match of the season, which was televised. When he made his debut at the Rose Bowl in the following week, he was accompanied by brass bands. Hampshire started in Division One by virtue of their finishing eighth in the Sunday League in 1998. However, they were relegated at the end of the summer and remained in Division Two for the next three years.

BENSON & HEDGES SUPER CUP

The Benson and Hedges competition departed from its normal format in 1999. There were no group stages and a knock-out competition was played instead. It was, though, confined to those teams who had finished in the top eight of the previous year's County Championship. Hampshire were comprehensively beaten by Yorkshire by nine wickets at Headingley in their only match. The normal B & H format was restored for the two remaining years of the competition's existence.

SOUTHAMPTON PLAYS HOST TO 1999 WORLD CUP

Southampton hosted two matches in the 1999 World Cup. The first match, between the West Indies and New Zealand, was played before a full house on a warm sunny day, with steel bands creating a carnival atmosphere. The former won by seven wickets, their match-winners being Mervyn Dillon (4-45) and Ridley Jacobs (80 not out). Dillon had previously played Southern League cricket for Trojans in the Southern League. The second match was played in cold, damp conditions before a more sparse crowd and resulted in Sri Lanka defeating Kenya by 45 runs. Maurice Odumbe scored 82 for the latter. The crowds over the two days had enjoyed a rare opportunity to watch such legends as Brian Lara, Sanath Jayasuriya and Aravinda de Silva.

SHANE WARNE'S DEBUT

Shane Warne made his Hampshire debut in a B & H group match at Chelmsford in April 2000. He had stepped off a plane from Australia earlier in the day and made his way to the ground immediately. The event was accompanied by the inevitable media scrum. Though he did not take a wicket, his inspirational presence resulted in a five-wicket victory for the county. Hampshire went on to reach the quarter-final for the only time between 1995 and 2002 but lost to Glamorgan at Cardiff.

EARLY FORTUNES AT THE ROSE BOWL

Unfortunately, the inaugural List A match at the Rose Bowl, against Essex in May 2001, in the B & H Cup, was abandoned without a ball being bowled. The ground was christened two days later in the same competition but Surrey spoiled the party by inflicting a 23-run defeat.

Hampshire had to wait a further nine days before they recorded their first victory, by three wickets against Worcestershire in the Norwich Union (formerly the National) League.

INTERNATIONAL CRICKET AT THE AGEAS BOWL

The Ageas Bowl staged its first international match in July 2003 when South Africa defeated Zimbabwe by seven wickets. The ground has now hosted 17 ODIs involving all the Test-playing nations: Australia (four times), Bangladesh (one), England (eleven), India (three), New Zealand (two), Pakistan (three), South Africa (two), Sri Lanka (one), and the West Indies (four). Zimbabwe (one), Kenya (one) and USA (one) have also played there. The Ageas Bowl hosted five matches in the ICC Champions Trophy in 2004. The only years in which the ground did not stage an ODI since 2003 were in 2005 and 2008. A Twenty20 International was awarded, however, in 2005. The match between New Zealand and the West Indies, which is included in the above figures, was abandoned without a ball being bowled. Ten of the eleven ODI matches played since 2006 have been day/night matches. : Twelve centuries have been scored by Ian Bell (two), Eoin Morgan (two), Alistair Cook, Andrew Flintoff and Jonathan Trott for England, Cameron White and Shane Watson for Australia, Younis Khan for Pakistan, Hashim Amla for South Africa and Martin Guptill for New Zealand.

Guptill's 189 not out in 2013 is the highest individual score and equalled Viv Richards' innings at Old Trafford in 1984 as the best by any player in a LOI in this country. The only two players to take five wickets in an innings are West Indies' Mervyn Dillon (5-29 v Bangladesh) in 2004 and England's Ben Stokes (5-60 v Australia) in 2013.

ONLY PLAYED AT BRISTOL

In 2004, after Michael Clarke had been selected to play for Australia in Zimbabwe early in the season, Hampshire signed another Aussie, Michael Dighton, as his temporary replacement. He played in two one-day matches against Gloucestershire at Bristol. He was engaged as a professional with Greenock in the Scotland National Cricket League at the time. Dighton scored 74 in a Totesport League match on debut and then 12 the following week in a C & G Trophy match. Clarke then rejoined the squad.

SHANE WATSON

The Australian Shane Watson made an astonishing impact when he played for Hampshire in 2004 and 2005. In the first of those years, he was signed by Hampshire for their Twenty20 squad. He came preciously close to becoming the first Hampshire player to score a century in the format when he raced to 97 not out off 68 balls against Kent Spitfires at the Rose Bowl. Two days later, he made his first-class debut for the county against Somerset at home, replacing the unavailable Shane Warne. He tore a hamstring but, batting with the aid of a runner, it did not stop him from scoring 112 not out in the second innings. In 2005, Watson replaced the New Zealander, Craig McMillan as an overseas signing in the second half of the season. He proceeded to play one of the best innings in Hampshire's one-day history, blasting 132 against Surrey at The Oval in the C & G Trophy. He was a member of Hampshire's winning side in the final. In the match immediately before the final, he had caned Warwickshire's bowling attack for 203 not out in a first-class match at the Rose Bowl.

LORD'S FINAL (4) – THE PRELUDE

Hampshire's fine victory in the C & G Trophy in 2005 emanated from sustained brilliance over a four-month period. It was all the more noteworthy as the first three matches were difficult encounters away from home, and achieved with constant changes of personnel. Hampshire first beat Shropshire by seven wickets at Whitchurch, before defeating Glamorgan at Cardiff by six wickets. It was in this match that Sean Ervine and Nic Pothas gave notice of the enormous influence they were to stamp on the competition. Ervine claimed 5-50 in Glamorgan's total of 214. Pothas scored 114 not out – his only one-day century for Hampshire. Kevin Pietersen had scored 76 and 69 not out in the two matches. All counties then had to wait two months for the quarter-finals, until after the Twenty20 regional rounds. By now, Shane Warne and Simon Katich had joined the Australian tour party and Pietersen was with the England one-day squad. The respective replacements were Australian Shane Watson, New Zealander Craig McMillan and the young Kevin Latouf. Billy Taylor replaced Richard Logan. Opponents Surrey had thrashed Hampshire by an innings, with Shane Warne present, in well under two days at the Rose Bowl a month earlier. The portents were not therefore propitious and that feeling was reinforced as Surrey posted a mammoth 358/6. When Hampshire batted they lost the first two wickets, including Pothas (27), for 41. They were also behind the scoring rate required. Watson, who had been unable to bowl in the Surrey innings because of a thigh strain, then hit a truly magnificent 132 off 115 balls (three sixes and 13 fours) which put the county so far ahead of the run rate that skipper Shaun Udal (44 not out) hit the winning run with 13 balls to spare and two wickets in hand. It was a famous victory and the confidence it inculcated was to sweep Hampshire through the semi-final against Yorkshire a month later at the Rose Bowl. In the meantime, McMillan had been replaced by Queenslander Andy Bichel. Jono McLean, the young South African batsman, replaced the luckless Taylor for the day. The ultimate eight-wicket victory was memorable for an illuminating innings of 100 off 90 balls by Ervine, and Hampshire's sensational fielding, which at times bordered on the supernatural. Pothas was again outstanding with the gloves and bat (73 not out). He and Ervine added 145 for the second wicket to take Hampshire to the brink of victory.

LORD'S FINAL (4)

Cheltenham and Gloucester Trophy – 3 September 2005
Hampshire 290 off 50 overs
(Sean Ervine 104, Nic Pothas 68; Neil Carter 5-66);
Warwickshire 272 off 49.2 overs
(Nick Knight 118; Shane Watson 3-34, Andy Bichel 3-57)
Hampshire won by 18 runs
Man of the match: Sean Ervine

Hampshire's only change from the semi-final side was Kevin Pietersen, released for the day by England, in for McLean. After losing the toss and being put into bat, Nic Pothas and John Crawley put on 57 for the first wicket before the latter was dismissed, gloving a hook to the wicketkeeper. Sean Ervine then almost replicated his innings against Yorkshire. He unfurled shots all around the wicket, with a judicious mixture of singles, twos and boundaries. His placement was excellent. After the pair had added 134 off only 20 overs, Pothas fell in the identical fashion to Crawley after scoring 68 off 99 balls. A total well in excess of 300 looked likely but then a succession of Hampshire players, including Ervine and Shane Watson, fell to catches on the boundary. It took a huge six, to the left of the pavilion, by Chris Tremlett to lift Hampshire to their eventual total of 290. Nick Knight and, more particularly Neil Carter, laid into Tremlett and Andy Bichel with a vengeance at the start of the Warwickshire innings. Carter heaved 32 off only 23 balls. Udal continually changed his bowlers but Knight and Ian Bell went efficiently about their business. The Hampshire captain had Bell dropped at mid-off but there were very few other alarms and it looked as if Warwickshire were going to stroll to victory. However, as he approached a cultured half-century, Bell began to suffer from cramp. It was at this stage that Udal threw the ball to Watson for a second spell. He simply roared in and Bell hit him to mid-off, where Tremlett gobbled up the chance. The door was now ajar and Watson and then Bichel swept through it, with great heart and passion. With Tremlett also catching the mood later, they demolished the remainder of the Warwickshire innings. Despite a late six-run penalty for a slow over rate, Hampshire emerged victorious by 18 runs. The three Hampshire pace bowlers had captured the last eight Warwickshire wickets for 68 in 12 overs.

SEAN ERVINE

Sean Ervine's first season with Hampshire was in 2005. He had, though, twice played at the Rose Bowl two years before with the touring Zimbabweans, one of the matches being the inaugural ODI at the ground. In Hampshire's C & G Trophy run, he had batted first wicket down. As his career has progressed the left-hander has usually batted at six, and earned a reputation in all forms of cricket as one of the world's best 'finishers'. In the four-day game he has often shepherded the tail to ensure a reasonable total. While making his maiden century for Hampshire, 103 not out against Lancashire at Old Trafford in 2007, he shared a last wicket stand of 53 with David Griffiths. Ervine scored all the runs. Against the same side at the Rose Bowl two years later, he battled his way to 114 out of the last 148 runs in Hampshire's innings. Three of his partners failed to score. Ervine's highest score of 237 not out against Somerset at the Rose Bowl included a reprise of his previous last wicket stand with Griffiths. In the summer of 2012, in making 109 not out against Glamorgan at the Rose Bowl, he and David Balcombe (39) put on 85 for the last wicket. Perhaps his finest innings, however, was his 94 not out against Durham at Basingstoke in 2008 when he steered Hampshire to victory as they successfully chased a victory target of 240, by far the highest total in the match, with two wickets in hand. Ervine has transferred the skill to limited-overs cricket also. His shrewd partnerships with Neil McKenzie in 2010 and with Simon Katich in 2012 were significant factors in both of Hampshire's Twenty20 triumphs, and success in the CB40 at Lord's in the latter year. He has been Hampshire's finest stroke maker in the last decade. Ervine is a very clean striker of the ball, with a penchant for hitting sixes. He is capable of changing the tenor of a match in very quick time. He has been a useful partnership breaker with his right-arm medium bowling. Prior to a serious knee injury shortly after the C & G Final in 2005, he was a brilliant fielder. He has never recovered that mobility but is a reliable catcher, particularly in the deep. In 2012, Ervine held the boundary catch that brought Hampshire a one-run victory at Chelmsford in the championship.

SHAUN UDAL

CHRIS TREMLETT IN ODIS

Chris Tremlett made a startling entry to international cricket in 2005. In the ODI against Bangladesh at Trent Bridge he removed Shariar Nafees and Tushar Imran in successive balls. Mohammad Ashraful then played the hat-trick ball on to his stumps, but it did not disturb the bails. Tremlett played in nine ODIs between 2005 and 2008 while with Hampshire, taking the same number of wickets. His debut figures of 4-32 remain both his best, and a record for any Hampshire bowler in ODIs.

PLAY-OFF

Hampshire were involved in English cricket's first play-off in September 2006. They enjoyed home advantage against Glamorgan to determine whether they would be promoted to Division One of the NatWest Pro 40 (National) League. If Glamorgan lost, they would be demoted from Division One. The match was decided by a fearless innings by Hampshire's Chris Benham. The Frimley-born right-handed batsman struck 158 (one six and 21 fours) off only 130 balls to take the county to 265/9. Glamorgan were dismissed for only 114, leaving Hampshire winners by 151 runs. Benham's is the highest one-day score by a Hampshire player against a first-class county at the Rose Bowl. Though he batted nervelessly in Hampshire's Friends Provident Final win against Sussex at Lord's in 2009, and went on to take 100 off a famously strong Durham bowling attack towards the end of the same season, he was unable to cement a place and was released at the end of the following season.

DIMITRI MASCARENHAS IN ODIS

Dimi Mascarenhas played in 20 ODIs between 2007 and September 2009, scoring 245 runs (average 22.27) and taking 13 wickets. The latter is a record for a Hampshire player in such matches. He enjoyed a wonderful series against India in 2007 when in successive matches, he scored 52 at Bristol, hit each of the last five balls in England's innings for six at The Oval, and returned ODI career best figures of 3-23 at Lord's. He had earlier become the first Hampshire player (leaving aside Kevin Pietersen) to play in an ODI at the Rose Bowl. He celebrated by capturing the prized wicket of Rahul Dravid.

LORD'S FINAL (5)

Friends Provident Trophy – 18 and 19 August 2007
Durham   312/5 off 50 overs (Shivnarine Chanderpaul 78, Dale
Benkenstein 61, Kyle Coetzer 61);
Hampshire 187 off 41 overs
(John Crawley 68; Ottis Gibson 3-24, Liam Plunkett 3-42; Paul
Collingwood 3-33)
Hampshire lost by 125 runs
Man of the match: Ottis Gibson

Hampshire lost their long unbeaten run of Lord's final successes when
they were overwhelmed by Durham by 125 runs. They outplayed
Hampshire at every turn as their game plan succeeded spectacularly.
Durham's batsmen played with such panache and élan, that not even
Shane Warne could stem the tide. Phil Mustard (49) set the tone at the
outset, tucking into all of Hampshire's bowlers with considerable relish.
By the time he was dismissed in the 13th over, the score stood at 69. Kyle
Coetzer (61) then took up the cudgels alongside the West Indian batsman,
Shivnarine Chanderpaul. After a hesitant start, the latter finessed the ball
all over Lord's. His touch and timing were exquisite. His innings was also
punctuated with unexpected bouts of violence as he twice pulled the ball
into the stands for huge sixes. Chanderpaul looked a certainty to reach a
century until he was run out by Michael Carberry when on 78. Upon their
dismissal, captain Dale Benkenstein (61 not out) and Ottis Gibson, who
hit his first two balls for four and six, took Durham to an imposing 312/5.
Hampshire's challenge was effectively still-born after the first two balls of
their innings. Gibson had taken all ten wickets in a championship match
against the county earlier in the season. He now induced Michael Lumb
to edge to Michael Di Venuto at second slip, as the ball was slanted across
him. His second ball was an action replay as Sean Ervine fell in identical
fashion. Increased cloud cover had made the pitch on which Durham had
thrived look a different proposition. Pietersen fell shortly afterwards,
again to Gibson, leg before to a ball which squatted. Thereafter, only
John Crawley (68), required to play a game foreign to his nature, Carberry
(23) and Nic Pothas (47) stayed for any time. Rain brought a premature
end to Saturday's play, and only a few hundred spectators were present as
Durham clinched victory in short order on Sunday morning.

THE WICKETKEEPERS

In 50 years of domestic one-day cricket, to the start of the 2013 season, 15 men have kept wicket for Hampshire in List A matches. In order of appearance they are: Colin Ingleby-Mackenzie (three matches), Brian Timms (nine), Bob Stephenson (237), Michael Hill (two), Bob Parks (244), Adi Aymes (221), Mark Garaway (two), Derek Kenway (32), Nic Pothas (128), Ian Brunnschweiler (two), John Crawley (two), Tom Burrows (nine), Michael Brown (four), Michael Bates (32) and Adam Wheater (12).

MOST DISMISSALS BY A WICKETKEEPER

Bob Parks (1980–1992) .... 303 ...... (260 caught, 43 stumped)
Adi Aymes (1987–2001) .... 268 ...... (215 caught, 53 stumped)
Bob Stephenson (1969–1980) ..... 249 ...... (191 caught, 58 stumped)
Nic Pothas (2002–2011) .... 151 ...... (120 caught, 31 stumped)

MOST DISMISSALS IN A SEASON

Bob Parks holds the Hampshire record with 39 victims in 1983. He caught 33 batsmen, another record. Bob Stephenson has claimed the most stumpings in a season – 11 in 1976.

MOST RUNS AND CENTURIES BY A WICKETKEEPER

Nic Pothas has, by far, the best record with the bat in List A matches. He scored 2,770 runs and his average, 35.97, is also unsurpassed. He is also the only wicketkeeper to score a century in List A matches. He scored two – 114 not out v Glamorgan at Cardiff in 2005 and 114 v Middlesex at the Rose Bowl in 2007. Michael Brown, standing in for the injured Pothas, came very close to emulating him when he finished on 96 not out against Worcestershire at the Rose Bowl in 2008.

AGAINST THE TOURISTS

Hampshire have played seven List A matches against touring sides: v West Indies in 1988 and 1995, v Pakistan A (1997), v Sri Lankan (1998), Zimbabwe (2003), v West Indies A (2006) and Bangladesh A (2013). They have a good record in such matches, winning four (West Indies in 1995, Zimbabwe, West Indies A and Bangladesh A) and losing two (West Indies in 1988 and Pakistan A). The match against the Sri Lankans was abandoned without a ball being bowled.

LORD'S FINAL (6)

Friends Provident Trophy – 18 and 19 August 2007
Sussex 219/9 off 50 overs (Michael Yardy 92 not out; Dominic Cork 4-41);
Hampshire 221/4 off 40.3 overs (Jimmy Adams 55; Luke Wright 3-50)
Hampshire won by six wickets
Man of the match: Dominic Cork

Hampshire's performance in this cup final was their most commanding of all their Lord's appearances. Sussex won the toss and elected to bat on a brown pitch which suggested dampness under the surface. They made their way to 30 after seven overs before Dominic Cork struck three times in 11 balls. Ed Joyce played on, Matt Prior was caught behind and Cork trapped Chris Nash leg before. Hampshire's control was reinforced by Chris Tremlett running out Murray Goodwin with a direct hit at the bowler's end from mid-off. He then bowled Luke Wright. Goodwin and Wright had generally prospered against Hampshire so Dimi Mascarenhas's team were in clover with Sussex on 77/5. However, the gritty Michael Yardy proceeded to play a captain's innings. He first received frenetic support from Dwayne Smith, and then more substantive and intelligent assistance from the young Rory Hamilton-Brown. The pair added 60 before the latter skied Tahir to Mascarenhas at midwicket. The Sussex innings eventually closed on 218/9 with Yardy 92 not out, while Cork's figures were 4-41. Hampshire's two openers, Jimmy Adams and Michael Lumb, set off rapaciously at five runs an over. All five of the Sussex mainline bowlers had turned their arm over by the 15th over. Adams was eventually trapped in front by Wright for 55 out of 93 in the 19th over. The latter then dismissed Lumb (38), caught at the wicket at 110. Sean Ervine and Michael Carberry continued in the same way before both perished hooking. With the score at 154/4, Sussex may have harboured thoughts of a further breakthrough. However, the massively reliable Nic Pothas and his partner, Chris Benham, both batted with élan. Hampshire never let up on dismantling the Sussex bowlers, even when Pothas suffered a recurrence of a groin injury when victory was in sight. The wicketkeeper pulled Hamilton-Brown high into the Mound Stand before Benham paddled the match-winning boundary to the leg side in front of the Tavern. The pair had put on 67 without any alarm.

DOMINIC CORK

Dominic Cork's man of the match award in that 2007 Friends Provident Final came 16 years after he had won one for Derbyshire in a Lord's final. On that occasion, it was for his batting when his 92 not out set a match-winning B & H Final total against Lancashire after his side were precariously placed. In his three years with Hampshire Cork became a folk hero. When the county signed him, many supporters were sceptical. His previous season with Lancashire hade been blighted by injury and he was approaching 37 years of age so his best days seemed to be behind him. And yet Cork had other ideas. He took 4-10 on debut against Worcestershire and continued in that manner. In 2010, on that magical evening under the Ageas Bowl lights, he captained Hampshire to victory in the Friends Provident Twenty20 Final against Somerset. With just one ball in the final over of their opponent's innings he made the critical contribution. Kieran Pollard, the big-hitting West Indian, who had clubbed 22 off just seven balls, was clearly unprepared for the bouncer which crashed between the grill and put him out of the match. Cork, always chivalrous, immediately called for medical assistance but the upshot was that Somerset scored only three runs off that over. The match finished with the scores tied but with Hampshire having lost fewer wickets. In his last match of his career at Twenty20 finals day at Edgbaston, Cork very nearly pulled the semi-final against Somerset out of the fire. Somerset looked to be sailing to victory but a marvellous last over by Cork, off which only four runs were scored, secured a tie. However, Hampshire were to lose in the 'eliminator over'. It was Cork's skill with both bat and ball, shrewd captaincy when he assumed the role in the latter part of the 2010 season, and his sheer enthusiasm that captured the imagination. Bending the ball like Beckham, he topped the bowling averages in both seasons. His calculated hitting changed the tempo of many innings, especially when Hampshire were in trouble. He took Hampshire's many youngsters, particularly James Vince, Michael Bates, Chris Wood, and Danny Briggs, under his wing in the Twenty20, and under his guidance, they thrived. If they continue to develop, he will have been instrumental in helping to set the foundations of a Hampshire side for the next decade. It is conceivable that England might benefit also. Cork fully justified Hampshire's faith in him, and in just three seasons became a living legend.

LORD'S FINAL (7)

CB40 Final – 15 September 2012
Hampshire 244/5 off 40 overs (Jimmy Adams 66, Sean Ervine 57);
Warwickshire 244/7 off 40 overs (Ian Bell 81; Chris Wood 3-39)
Hampshire won by virtue of losing fewer wickets
Man of the match: Jimmy Adams

Hampshire were without Danny Briggs, who was with the England Twenty20 squad in Sri Lanka, and Dimi Mascarenhas who was nursing a shoulder injury, though they had flown Neil McKenzie back from South Africa for the occasion. Warwickshire started clear favourites having won the County Championship. And yet Hampshire prevailed. When Neil Carter hit the penultimate ball from Kabir Ali to the extra cover boundary to level the scores, a Warwickshire victory seemed inevitable. However, Ali then bowled a low full toss which Carter missed. Michael Bates, brilliant all day, snaffled the ball but just to make sure that a run was not stolen, both whipped off the bails and then with Carter now out of his ground lifted a stump out with the ball in his hand. Hampshire had won their sixth Lord's final out of seven attempts. They had played outstandingly throughout. Batting after losing the toss, Michael Carberry and James Vince seemed to be on the verge of giving a reprise of their semi-final fireworks of Hove (when they opened with 126 off 79 balls). When the latter found Patel on the midwicket boundary they had added 48 off 41 balls. Carberry (35 off 31 balls) had launched two sixes over mid-on, as well as a fierce straight-driven boundary. After he perished at 70, the innings lost momentum for a while, though Jimmy Adams was working the ball intelligently around the field. It was a largely unobtrusive innings and yet he reached 51 off the same number of balls, shortly after McKenzie (19) was bowled by Ian Blackwell. He eventually made a polished 66. Sean Ervine (57) and Simon Katich (35 not out) then put on 69 for the fifth wicket. Hampshire's four left-handers had delivered a masterclass. In Warwickshire's reply, Hampshire found the happy knack of taking wickets at crucial moments. Warwickshire retained wickets in hand but with five overs remaining they still required another 52 runs. Ian Bell (81) provided his side with much needed acceleration but when he struck a full toss from David Griffiths to the remarkable Carberry, whose fielding was on a different level to any other man on the day.

It seemed as if Hampshire now held the advantage but thanks to some shrewd blows by Chris Woakes off Chris Wood's final over, seven were required off the last over. However, by now, Warwickshire had lost six wickets and a seventh went when Kabir clean bowled Blackwell with the second ball of his last over. His last ball will undoubtedly earn him a permanent niche in the county's history. Jimmy Adams was named man of the match for his batting, two catches and, above all, his captaincy. He held his nerve wonderfully in those last five overs when Warwickshire made their victory dash.

MOST APPEARANCES IN A LORD'S FINAL

Forty-six players played for Hampshire in their seven Lord's finals between 1988 and 2012. Sean Ervine, with four, has made the most appearances. Ten men played on three occasions: Paul Terry, Robin Smith, Jon Ayling, Cardigan Connor, Shaun Udal, Nic Pothas, Dimitri Mascarenhas, Chris Tremlett and Michael Carberry. Udal's final two appearances were 13 years apart (1992–2005).

CAPTAINS IN A LORD'S FINAL

Six men have captained Hampshire in Lord's finals: Mark Nicholas (1998 and 1992), David Gower (1991), Shaun Udal (2005), Shane Warne (2007), Dimi Mascarenhas (2009) and Jimmy Adams (2012).

MAN OF THE MATCH AWARDS IN LORD'S FINALS

Six Hampshire players have also won man of the match awards: Steve Jefferies (1988), Robin Smith (1991 and 1992), Sean Ervine (2005), Dominic Cork (2009) and Jimmy Adams (2012).

YOUNGEST DEBUTANT

Off-spin bowler Brad Taylor became the youngest player to appear for Hampshire in a List A match in the encounter with Bangladesh A at the Ageas Bowl on 6 August 2013. He was 16 years 145 days old. He became the county's youngest debutant in the County Championship when he took the field against Lancashire at Liverpool 22 days later.

TWENTY20 – A BRIEF HISTORY

Hampshire took some time to get to grips with Twenty20 cricket. In the first seven seasons following the introduction of the format in 2003 they finished bottom of their group twice, and progressed beyond the group stage on only two occasions. They possessed the worst record of any county in those seven years. However, in the last four seasons (2010–2013), the team have enjoyed remarkable success, winning the competition twice and losing twice in the semi-finals. As a result of their two trophy-winning performances, Hampshire participated in the West Indies Regional Tournament in 2010/11 and the Champions League in 2012.

COMPETITION RESULTS

In the period 2003–2013, Hampshire have played 121 matches in the T20 competition. They have won 64, lost 45 and tied twice. There have been eight no results. In domestic T20 cricket their win record of 59.90 per cent is exceeded only by Lancashire (60.28). Hampshire have played against all the other counties except Derbyshire.

INAUGURAL MATCH

Hampshire staged the very first match in county cricket's Twenty20 competition. They played the Sussex Sharks at the Rose Bowl on 13 June 2003, defeating the visitors by five runs. Some 9,000 people watched the game, many of whom stayed on for the musical concert that followed. The match was also televised. Unfortunately, Hampshire failed to win another match and finished at the foot of their group.

FIRST HAT-TRICK

Dimitri Mascarenhas claimed the first hat-trick by any bowler in Twenty20 cricket against Sussex under the floodlights at Hove in July 2004. In damp conditions and on a pitch that assisted seam bowlers he was virtually unplayable as he took 5-14 in 23 balls. All three of his hat-trick victims, Mark Davis, Mushtaq Ahmed and Jason Lewry, were dismissed playing defensively so the wickets were earned, and not thrown away. It was also the first time a Hampshire bowler had taken five wickets in a T20 innings, a feat since equalled by Shahid Afridi and Danny Briggs. His analysis remains the best by a Hampshire bowler in the competition.

NEW VENUES

Twenty20 cricket has taken Hampshire to two venues for the first time, Beckenham (2003 and 2006) in Kent and Old Deer Park, Richmond (2005, 2008 and 2012-2013). Although the latter is situated in Surrey, Middlesex have played there in Twenty20 matches. Somewhat quirkily, Hampshire have won all of their four matches at Richmond but lost both at Beckenham.

CONTROVERSIAL RUN OUT

In Hampshire's match against Sussex at Arundel in 2006, future England star Matt Prior was run out controversially. He appeared to be walking off to change his gloves but Chris Benham threw down the stumps at the bowler's end, whereupon Prior was given out.

THREE STUMPINGS IN AN INNINGS

When Twenty20 cricket started, it was generally assumed that stumpings would be few and far between. However, Nic Pothas effected three stumpings in an innings four times and Derek Kenway and Michael Bates each did so once.

CROWD TROUBLE

Despite the increased tribalism brought about by Twenty20 cricket, virtually all matches have been free of crowd trouble. A notable exception was Hampshire's match against Middlesex at Southgate in 2007. Though the home side won the match, items were stolen from their dressing room and stones were thrown at the windows of the coach carrying the Hampshire team away from the ground.

TORMENTED BY FORMER CAPTAIN

Former Hampshire captain Shaun Udal tormented his old county in 2008, the season after his departure, when he played for his new club Middlesex. On his return to the Rose Bowl he scored 32 not out off 18 balls (three sixes) and took 3-31. It was the decisive factor in Middlesex's 33-run victory. In the return at Richmond he conceded just 11 runs in his four overs and claimed the vital wicket of Dimi Mascarenhas, then hit four sixes in his 40 not out. However, on this occasion, Hampshire prevailed by six runs. Udal won the man of the match award in both encounters.

FIRST FINALS DAY AT THE ROSE BOWL

The Rose Bowl hosted their first Twenty20 finals day in 2008. It was a hugely successful occasion, blessed by fine weather, a sell-out crowd and excellent organisation. Kent, Essex, Durham and Middlesex were the four counties to appear on the day. Kent accounted for Essex by 14 runs in the first semi-final before Middlesex defeated Durham more easily by eight wickets in the second. In an enthralling final with fortunes ebbing and flowing throughout, Middlesex (187/6) just held off Kent (184/5) by three runs. In the words of the *Hampshire Handbook*, Shaun Udal (now of Middlesex) was 'afforded a wonderful reception and played splendidly'. He had taken two wickets and conceded only 39 runs in his eight overs on the day.

PINK BALL EXPERIMENT

Towards the end of the 2008 season, Hampshire and Essex played each other home and away in a Twenty20 Floodlit Cup, part of the purpose of which was to allow an experiment with a pink ball. Each side won their home matches but Hampshire took the trophy on overall run rate. Pink balls have still to be introduced in matches between counties in England.

TIED MATCHES

Hampshire have been involved in two tied matches. On both occasions they were played under the Rose Bowl lights, against Kent in 2007 and Essex in 2008.

HAMPSHIRE'S FIRST CENTURY

Michael Lumb scored Hampshire's first century in Twenty20 cricket against Essex at the Rose Bowl in 2009. He blitzed 124 not out (14 fours and four sixes) off only 69 balls, sharing a second wicket partnership of 170 with Michael Carberry (62). He brought up his first 50 off 30 balls and required only a further 26 balls to reach 100. Lumb's score and the partnership remain Hampshire records. At the time it was the fourth highest individual innings by a batsman in Twenty20 cricket. In the next two matches Lumb charged to 59 against Kent at Tunbridge Wells and, on the following day, 93 against Middlesex at the Rose Bowl. On the latter occasion he reached 50 off 31 balls.

ONLY PLAYED FOR HAMPSHIRE IN TWENTY20

Five men have played for Hampshire in Twenty20 matches without appearing for the county in any other form of cricket: Adam Voges (2007), Ian Harvey (2008), Abdul Razzaq (2010), Shahid Afridi (2011), and Glenn Maxwell (2012). They were all overseas players; Voges, Harvey and Maxwell being from Australia, and Razzaq and Afridi from Pakistan.

MOST APPEARANCES

Sean Ervine has made 96 appearances for Hampshire in Twenty20 cricket, the most by any player. He is followed by Jimmy Adams (91), Nic Pothas (79), Dimitri Mascarenhas (74), Michael Carberry (67), Danny Briggs 63 and James Vince (62).

MOST RUNS

Perhaps not surprisingly, Ervine has scored most T20 runs – 1,864. Five other players have passed 1000 runs – Michael Carberry (1808), Jimmy Adams (1747), James Vince (1425) and Neil McKenzie (1289).

MOST WICKETS

Dimitri Mascarenhas has claimed 94 T20 wickets. He is followed by Danny Briggs (80), Chris Wood (54), Sean Ervine (47) and Dominic Cork (43)

MOST CATCHES

James Vince (43) has held most catches by an outfield player. He is followed by the ubiquitous Ervine (37).

HIGHEST INNINGS TOTAL

Hampshire's highest innings total in T20 is 225/2 against Middlesex at the Rose Bowl in 2006. Michael Carberry (90 off 59 balls) and Mitchell Stokes (62 off 39) shared an opening stand of 122 in 12 overs. The Australian Dominic Thornely then struck 50 not out off just 21 balls (two fours and four sixes) and Dimi Mascarenhas cleared the ropes with the only two balls he received. For Stokes, a 19-year-old right-handed batsman from Basingstoke, it was the highest score of his career for Hampshire. He was released at the end of the season having played only in Twenty20 cricket and List A matches.

LOWEST INNINGS TOTAL

Hampshire were bowled out for 85 in 18.4 overs by Sussex at the Rose Bowl in 2008. Michael Lumb top scored with 32. Four wickets fell with the score at 43, with Michael Carberry, Chris Benham and Sean Ervine all dismissed without scoring. The chief executioner was left-arm fast-medium bowler Chris Liddle, who was making his Twenty20 debut for Sussex.

THE WICKETKEEPERS

Four men, Nic Pothas, Derek Kenway, Michael Bates and Adam Wheater have kept wicket in Twenty20 matches. Pothas claimed 47 dismissals (33 caught and 14 stumped), Bates 20 (14/6), Kenway 5 (2/3) and Wheater 5 (3/2).

THE ALL ROUNDERS

Three men have scored more than 300 runs and taken over 30 wickets in Twenty20 cricket for Hampshire: Sean Ervine (1864 runs/47 wickets), Dimitri Mascarenhas (732/94) and Liam Dawson (328/30).

DIMITRI MASCARENHAS – PATHFINDER

Hampshire's engaging and charismatic all-rounder Dimitri Mascarenhas has been a pathfinder in other Twenty20 tournaments in the world. He was the first county cricketer to gain a contract in the IPL when he played for the Rajasthan Royals between 2008 and 2010. The Royals were captained by Shane Warne and included Shane Watson who appeared for Hampshire with marked success in 2004 and 2005. Mascarenhas was followed by Michael Lumb. He then played for Kings XI, Punjab, in 2012. He was also the first county cricketer to play Twenty20 cricket in New Zealand. Mascarenhas dovetailed his IPL commitments with appearances for Otago (2009 and 2011/12) and for Wellington in the current winter. Jimmy Adams was subsequently recruited by Auckland. Mascarenhas was also the first Hampshire man to appear in the Champions League when he played for Otago in the 2009 version in South Africa. The downside to his Twenty20 activities was that he became less available for Hampshire. Injuries have also curtailed his appearances. However, his shrewd captaincy and experience in the format was a crucial part of the county's Twenty20 title success in 2012. He has captained Hampshire on most occasions – 30 – in the format. He retired last summer. Strangely for a man who enjoyed an 18-year career and played Twenty20 cricket in five different countries, all of his 195 first-class matches were for Hampshire.

DANNY BRIGGS

Danny Briggs claimed a Hampshire record 31 wickets (averaging 14.35) in Twenty20 cricket in 2010. It was an extraordinary performance by the 19-year-old slow left-arm spin bowler from the Isle of Wight, in his debut season in the competition. He took a wicket every 13 balls. His tally included figures of 4-0-5-3 against Kent at Canterbury, which included a wide. He then enjoyed an impressive winter in the West Indies with the England Lions in the regional first-class tournament. He took more wickets than any other bowler – 33 (average 18.87). Briggs collected career best figures of 6-45 against Windward Islands at Roseau. He then bowled a marathon spell of 45 overs against Jamaica at Kingston, to take 5-121 in the first innings, and took 4-56 in the second. His efforts just failed to secure the match and the championship. Briggs then enjoyed another fine Twenty20 season in 2011 – 23 wickets, including 5-19 against Durham at the Rose Bowl in the quarter-finals. Again his average (14.91) and strike rate (13 balls per wicket, as in 2010) were eye-catching. These consistent performances resulted in his promotion to the England limited overs squad. Briggs made his international bow in an ODI against Pakistan in Dubai in February 2012, in which he performed very creditably with figures of 2-39 in ten overs. Though he found wickets harder to come by in all forms of cricket in 2012, he was selected for three international Twenty20 matches in the autumn, including a World Cup appearance against New Zealand in Sri Lanka. He has retained his place in ENgland's Twenty20 squad since. Such has been his rapid progress that it is easy to forget that he was still only 22 years old at the time of writing, and some setbacks may still lie ahead. He is still regarded predominantly as a limited overs specialist but when called upon to play a full season of four-day matches for Hampshire in 2011, he took more wickets (38) than any other bowler. After Derek Underwood, he is the youngest spin bowler to take 100 wickets in his career.

MOST RUNS IN A SEASON

In 2010, Jimmy Adams set a new record for the number of runs scored by any player in a Twenty20 season. In 19 matches he struck 668 runs (average 39.29) at the handsome strike rate of 132.2 per 100 balls. This tally included two unbeaten centuries, both at the Rose Bowl – 101 v Surrey and 100 v Glamorgan. He had appeared for his club, St. Cross, in the Southern Premier League on the day before the first of those innings. Perhaps, though, the best of his knocks was an intelligent 61 against Somerset at the Rose Bowl on a treacherous, indeed dangerous, pitch which had been relaid. No other Hampshire batsman made double figures, or looked interested in staying at the wicket. The county were chasing only 105 to win but fell seven runs short. Hampshire were fined two points for their 2011 campaign for the condition of the pitch.

TWENTY20 CHAMPIONS 2010

On a night unsurpassed for emotion and tension, Hampshire triumphed in the Friends Provident Twenty20 Final when they defeated Somerset off the last ball at the Rose Bowl on Saturday 14 August 2010. The scores were level but Hampshire won by virtue of losing fewer wickets. They thus became the first, and so far, only, county to win the competition on their own ground. Hampshire's ultimate victory was against immense odds. Seven senior players – Kabir Ali, Dimitri Mascarenhas, Simon Jones, Nic Pothas, Michael Lumb, Shahid Afridi and Kevin Pietersen – were either injured or absent for all or part of the campaign. However, four 19-year-old replacements – Danny Briggs, Chris Wood, James Vince and Michael Bates – as well as Australian Dan Christian filled the voids so ably so that there was little, if any, discussion about their injured team-mates. Hampshire defeated Sussex, the holders, at the Rose Bowl to qualify for the quarter-finals, where they accounted for Warwickshire thanks to telling contributions from captain Dominic Cork, Briggs (three wickets) and Vince (66 not out). The first opponents on finals day were Essex who had twice beaten Hampshire in the group stages and famously recruited Dwayne Bravo at an alleged cost of between £8,000 and £10,000 for the day. However, Cork's side were now ready for anybody.

A rapid first wicket stand of 79 between Mark Pettini and Alastair Cook appeared to put Essex in firm control before Briggs intervened. He took three quick wickets as well as catching Cook on the boundary. Essex limped to 156/7, Bravo making only five. As at Edgbaston, Adams and Abdul Razzaq littered the early part of the innings with boundaries. Sean Ervine continued in the same vein before Neil McKenzie and Michael Carberry took Hampshire to victory by six wickets. Favourites Somerset awaited them in the final. They, too, had defeated Hampshire twice in the group stages. Razzaq accounted for Marcus Trescothick early on. Though his opening partner Craig Kieswetter eventually made 73, the runs took him a long time. Only when Kieron Pollard came to the wicket three overs from the end did Somerset threaten to post an unassailable total. The irrepressible Cork then conceded only three runs in the final over as well as taking a wicket and putting Pollard out of the game when a ball got stuck in the grill of the latter's helmet. Somerset finished at 173/6. Hampshire seemed to be in cruise control after an opening partnership of 60 between Adams and Razzaq, and as Neil McKenzie and Sean Ervine serenely constructed a fourth wicket partnership of 79. However, after the former's dismissal at 163 with 11 balls remaining, the atmosphere changed dramatically. With two balls left, three runs were still required. Christian then seemed to have won the match as he swung to midwicket. However, brilliant fielding saved the boundary and restricted the score to two. Two runs were now notionally required though Hampshire would still win the game if they managed only a single, by virtue of losing fewer wickets. The final ball took five minutes to be delivered. Christian had pulled a hamstring and required a runner. Trescothick, not unreasonably given the circumstances, asked for creases to be painted where Jimmy Adams (the runner) was to be located. The last ball struck Christian on the pads. As Somerset appealed, Ervine ran to the business end and Christian, forgetting his injury, left his crease (he would have been run out had the Somerset fielders the presence of mind to throw the wicket down) and made it to the bowler's end to begin a night of wild celebrations for Hampshire players and supporters alike.

Somerset Sabres 173/6 (Kieswetter 71; Cork 2-24, Razzaq 2-37); Hampshire Royals 173/5 (McKenzie 52, Ervine 44 not out; Phillips 2-44)
Man of the match: Neil McKenzie

ADAMS'S THREE FINALS IN SIX MONTHS

Jimmy Adams played in three Twenty20 Finals on three different continents in the space of six months in 2010/11. First, he played for Hampshire in the domestic success at the Rose Bowl in August 2010. He then helped Auckland win the HRV Cup in New Zealand in early January 2011 before captaining his county in the Caribbean Twenty20 Final against Trinidad and Tobago in Bridgetown, Barbados, three weeks later.

FINALISTS IN THE CARIBBEAN

After their success in 2010, Hampshire were invited to participate in the Caribbean Twenty20 tournament in January 2011. Due to commitments elsewhere or injury, Hampshire were without Michael Lumb, Neil McKenzie, Dominic Cork, Abdul Razzaq and Michael Carberry from their trophy-winning side, but still reached the final. They lost to Canada in the first match but then defeated Barbados, Leeward Islands and the Windward Islands en route to the final. The match against Barbados was a nail-biter, Hampshire eventually gaining victory in the Super Over as the scores were level after 20 overs. It was the first time the county had been involved in such an event. In the qualifying stages there was also a no result after rain interrupted the fixture against their opponents in the final, Trinidad and Tobago. The latter were to prove too strong for Hampshire's young side, seven of whom were 22 or under, winning by 36 runs.

JOHANN MYBURGH

In the Caribbean Twenty20 tournament, South African Johann Myburgh twice hit six sixes in an innings as he made 77 off 57 balls against Leeward Islands at the Sir Vivian Richards Stadium in Antigua and 88 off 58 versus the Windward Islands at Bridgetown. Hampshire signed Myburgh for the ensuing summer but, despite many promising starts to an innings, he never came to terms with the requirements of county cricket. He was not selected for any matches in Hampshire's Twenty20 domestic campaign. His brother-in-law Friedel de Wet, who had previously played with some success in two Tests for South Africa against England in 2009/10, was also signed for the summer and he too proved similarly disappointing.

BEATEN SEMI-FINALISTS IN 2011

In 2011, Hampshire played with marvellous assurance throughout the group stages. Notwithstanding starting the season with a two-point deduction, they topped the group for the first and, so far, only time. They did so with ease, winning 11 of their 13 completed matches. They then brushed aside Durham by 55 runs in the quarter-finals at the Rose Bowl to reach finals day for the second successive year. On this occasion, Edgbaston hosted the event. In a spooky re-run of their final against Somerset 12 months earlier, Hampshire fell in the semi-finals against the same county. Again, the scores finished level but on this occasion, an 'elimination over' was bowled. In a match interrupted continually by rain, Hampshire totalled 138/4 off 15.5 overs, with Shahid Afridi scoring an illuminating 80. The Duckworth-Lewis formula meant that Somerset required 95 to win in ten overs. After posting 40 off the first three, a Somerset victory looked a formality. However, Hampshire pegged them back and Dominic Cork, in his swansong for the county, conceded only four runs off his last over. Arul Suppiah was run out off the final ball by James Vince as he attempted the winning run. However, in the eliminator, Shahid Afridi was unable to reprise his earlier effort and Hampshire scored only five runs against Somerset's 16.

GLENN MAXWELL

The 22-year-old Australian all-rounder, Glenn Maxwell, took the cricket world by storm in the group stages of the 2012 Twenty20 tournament. He was drafted into the Hampshire side after savaging Southern League bowling attacks while playing for South Wilts. He first came to attention on the county scene by clubbing 66 not out (six sixes and five fours) off 32 balls v Kent at Canterbury. He then raced to 60 not out (four sixes and six fours) off only 24 balls against Essex at Chelmsford, striking the luckless Tim Phillips for 30 (4-6-4-6-6-4) in one over en route. Maxwell ensured Hampshire won both matches from tricky situations. Unfortunately, he missed the final stages as he was called up by Australia's selectors for their Twenty20 squad against Pakistan in the UAE. In the winter of 2012/13 he was playing under Shane Warne's captaincy for the Melbourne Stars in Australia's Big Bash. Maxwell was also the first Hampshire player to wear red cricket shoes!

TWENTY20 CHAMPIONS 2012

After obtaining only one point from their first three matches, Hampshire needed to avoid any further losses. Partly thanks to Maxwell's pyrotechnics, they did so. The quarter-final at Trent Bridge looked daunting. Nottinghamshire had inflicted Hampshire's first defeat in the CB40 competition a week earlier. However, thanks to a genius-laden unbeaten 79 from Neil McKenzie, Hampshire emerged victorious from a match in which Notts always seemed to have their noses in front. On finals day at the SWALEC Stadium in Cardiff, Hampshire had to play Somerset yet again in the semi-finals. With Marcus Trescothick returning from injury,

Somerset were overwhelming favourites. As in the encounters in the previous years, however, the Hampshire bowlers, especially Mascarenhas, Ervine and Briggs, checked the Somerset stroke players, apart from Kieswetter. He was on 63 when the innings ended at 124/6. This time, Hampshire's batsmen ensured there would be no close finish. Though they were 72/4, the season's two best finishers, Simon Katich (32) and Sean Ervine (34), then steered them home without any further alarm with an over to spare. Yorkshire awaited in the final. Hampshire were again second favourites. Hampshire had turned the run chase into an art form during their progress so it was a new challenge for them to bat first. The only other occasion they had done so was in their defeat to Middlesex in their first completed match of the season. Cameos by Jimmy Adams (43), James Vince (36), Ervine (25) and Katich (21) enabled Hampshire to post 150/6, which was regarded as a competitive total. Canny bowling changes by Mascarenhas kept the Yorkshire batting on its toes. None was able to make headway apart from the South African David Miller. He launched a furious assault on Ervine in particular to bring Yorkshire into contention. They required 21 off the last two overs. The Hampshire captain then entrusted the penultimate over to Briggs. He bowled quite nervelessly, conceding only six. Mascarenhas threw the ball to Chris Wood, who induced Tim Bresnan to sky to Ervine at cover off the first ball. Wood then bowled three yorkers to Miller and Richard Pyrah and 11 were required off the last two balls. Wood duly castled Pyrah with another yorker and had Azeem Rafiq caught off the final ball, again by Ervine, at extra cover.

Hampshire 150/6 (Adams 43; Sidebottom 2-20); Yorkshire 140/8 (Miller 72 not out; Wood 3-26, Mascarenhas 2-20)
Hampshire won by ten runs

HAMPSHIRE IN THE CHAMPIONS LEAGUE

Having won the domestic Twenty20 competition, Hampshire were rewarded with a place in the Champions League in South Africa in October 2012. However, with little time for preparation after the end of the county season, and denuded of Simon Katich and Neil McKenzie, who were playing for rival teams in the competition, and Danny Briggs with the England squad, they did not progress beyond the qualifying round. Though they were able to call upon Shahid Afridi and Glenn Maxwell, they were defeated by Auckland at Centurion Park and the Sialkot Stallions in Johannesburg.

ENGLAND'S FIRST TWENTY20 MATCH

The Rose Bowl (as it was then called) staged England's first ever Twenty20 international match on 13 June 2005. Their opponents were Australia who were overwhelmed by 100 runs. After England posted 179/8 in their 20 overs (Paul Collingwood 46, Marcus Trescothick 41; Glenn McGrath 3-31), Australia subsided to 31/7 in reply before England's opening bowling attack of Darren Gough (3-16) and Jonathan Lewis (4-24). At this point, the sell-out crowd of 14,097 were singing, 'Are you Bangladesh in disguise?' Australia were eventually dismissed for 79 in only 14.3 overs (Jason Gillespie 24). Only three batsmen made double figures. The crowd were doing Bangladesh a disservice as they beat Australia by five wickets in an ODI five days later.

AN INTERNATIONAL THRILLER

The second Twenty20 international match at the Rose Bowl on 15 June 2006 was a thriller. Sri Lanka batted on winning the toss and made a flying start as Sanath Jayasuriya (41) and Upal Tharanga (34) thumped 75 off the first eight overs. Paul Collingwood (4-22) then applied the brakes and they were dismissed for 163 off the last ball. Marcus Trescothick and Andrew Strauss (33) saw England on their way with an opening stand of 59. The former seemed to have victory within England's reach when he hit Malinga for three fours in the 18th over. However, after he was run out for 73 with eight balls remaining and 12 required, the remaining England batsmen were unable to bridge the gap. Sri Lanka squeezed home by two runs as England finished on 161/5.

QUICKEST VICTORY

The crowd at Bristol on 19 June 2010 might have been excused for asking for their money to be returned. Hampshire bowled out Gloucestershire for 68 in 17.5 overs, Sean Ervine returning career best Twenty20 figures of 4-12. Only two batsmen recorded double figures. Hampshire then knocked off the runs in 7.3 overs for the loss of three wickets. The whole game therefore lasted 25.2 overs, 63 per cent of the scheduled playing time. It is the quickest victory in the history of the competition.

LOST IN TWO SEMI-FINALS

After winning both the Twenty20 and CB 40 finals in 2012, Hampshire again excelled in the corresponding competitions in 2013. The county's progress to their fourth successive finals day in the Twenty20 competition was inexorable. They lost only match en route. However, they then bowed out to Surrey in the semis by four wickets. Hampshire must regard Edgbaston as a hoodoo ground on finals day. Both of their semi-final defeats have occurred there. Without the hugely influential Michael Carberry, they lost to Glamorgan in the semi-finals of the YB40 tournament by 31 runs at the Ageas Bowl.

WORLD RECORD INNINGS IN T20 INTERNATIONALS

When playing for Australia against England at the Ageas Bowl at the end of August 2013, Aaron Finch played, indisputably, the most astonishing innings hitherto in T20 international cricket. He belted 156 off just 63 balls, 128 of his runs coming in boundaries. Most of his 14 sixes cleared the 85-yard boundary by the proverbial country mile. Australia amassed 248 for six. Despite an unbeaten 90 from Joe Root, England fell short by 39 runs.

NEIL MCKENZIE

Neil McKenzie averaged a staggering 100.33 in the domestic Twenty20 tournament in 2013. The fact that he was dismissed only three times in 13 innings in scoring 301 runs exemplifies his unique abilities as a "finisher". Many Hampshire followers will come to regard him as the ultimate performer in the format. His timing, placement and judgement of the required pace of an innings were wondrous. He was above the normal helter-skelter of Twenty20 cricket. He gathered his runs with subtlety, skill and intelligence. He was with Hampshire for four years from 2010-2013. The county reached Twenty20 finals in each of those years and he was Man of the Match in the 2010 final at the Ageas Bowl. His contribution was simply immense. He was also a man of idiosyncrasies. He taped his bat to the ceiling whilst waiting to go in. When running between the wickets he also carried his bat in a manner which suggested that fielders may steal it away from him. In the first-class game he has a share in county cricket's record third wicket partnership (see page 30). He will be much missed.

MICHAEL CARBERRY (2)

In 2013, Michael Carberry scored Hampshire's fourth century in Twenty20 cricket with an unbeaten 100 not out(off 66 balls) against Lancashire at the Ageas Bowl in the quarter-finals. A few weeks earlier he had slammed a resplendent 150 not out in 115 balls against the same opponents in the YB40 competition at the Ageas Bowl. These performances earned him a call to England's limited-overs squad against Ireland and Australia. He went on to play in five ODIs, making 63 against the latter at Cardiff. He impressed to such an extent that England thrust him into the Ashes squad for the forthcoming tour of Australia. He scored more runs on the tour than any other batsman and was second in run aggregate in the test series to Kevin Pietersen. Given the fact that he is arguably the most punitive batsman in domestic cricket in both shortened forms of the game, it seemed strange that England did not select him to play in any of the ODIs and Twenty20 matches at the end of the tour.

BANGLADESH PREMIER LEAGUE

Sean Ervine and Kabir Ali broke new ground in 2011/12 when they appeared in the newly established Bangladesh Premier League. Their two sides, Duronto Rajshahi and Barisol Burners respectively, met in the semi-final. The latter won the encounter but not before Ervine had scored a Twenty20 best of 82 – and was run out by his Hampshire team-mate. One of Ervine's colleagues was Abdul Razzaq with whom he played in Hampshire's Twenty20 title-winning side of 2010. Barisol Burners eventually lost the final to Dhaka Gladiators by eight wickets. Interestingly, Kabir had not yet played for Hampshire in Twenty20 cricket. He went on to play in four matches in 2011 and one match in the Champions League before signing for Lancashire for the 2013 season. Dimitri Mascarenhas played one match in the BPL in 2013/13, and Liam Dawson went on to play in the Dhaka Premier League in 2013/14.

SEAN ERVINE IN ZIMBABWE

Sean Ervine has played for three teams in his native Zimbabwe. His evocatively named sides have been Southern Rocks (2009/10), Mountaineers (2010/11) and Matabeleland Tuskers (2011/12).

FIRST TO PLAY IN AUSTRALIA

Ervine was also the first Hampshire player to appear in Australia's Twenty20 Big Bash when he played for Western Australia in 2006/07 and 2007/08.

INDIAN CRICKET LEAGUE

Nic Pothas was one of the few county cricketers to appear in this league when he played for Delhi Giants in March 2008. While the league pre-dated the IPL, it lacked the support of the Indian authorities and folded in 2009. Former Hampshire players Trevor Jesty and Nigel Cowley both officiated as umpires in the ICL.

FIRST WOMEN'S COUNTY MATCH

The first women's county match took place between Hampshire and Surrey in October 1811. The Hampshire side won by an innings. Those who played in Hampshire's side demand mention: Sarah Luff, Mary Pulain, Hannah Parker, Elizabeth Smith, Martha Smith, Mary Woodrow, Mary Hislock, Nancy Porter, Ann Poulters, Mary Nowell and Mary Jougan.

HAMPSHIRE WOMEN

Following the match in 1811, the next reference to a Hampshire women's team is in 1935. Unfortunately details of scores, the result and venue of the game are unknown. The county first played against a touring side when they entertained Australia Women in Winchester on 7 July 1937. The one-day match was drawn. This is the last reference to 'Hampshire Women' until 1997, when they played Middlesex Women Second XI at Eversley. Hampshire Women have played in the Women's County Championship, a limited-overs competition, since 1997 as follows: 1997–2002 Division Three; 2003–2004 Division Two; 2005 Division Three; 2008 Division Four; 2009–2010 Division Three; 2011 Division Four; 2012–2013 Division Three.

Between 1997 and 2004 all the matches were played in a five-day tournament on the Cambridge University College grounds. The highest score for Hampshire in these matches was 97 not out by Natasha Raine v Devon at Blundell's School in 2009. The best bowling return was 6-17 by Kerry Hartnett v Lancashire at Yateley in 2010.

MAY'S BOUNTY, BASINGSTOKE

Hampshire first played host to an international women's match in 1937 when the Australian Women came to Basingstoke to play West Women. The home side batted first and totalled 218, 35-year-old Amy Bull scoring 117. This was the last major match in which Bull played. She later became president of the Women's Cricket Association between 1964 and 1970. However, the Australians went on to win by eight wickets with Patricia Holmes scoring 200, before 'retiring out'.

This is the highest individual score in women's matches in the county. The West side included Betty Snowball, who with Molly Hide was one of the star women players in the 1930s and 1940s.

DEAN PARK, BOURNEMOUTH

Australia Women played West Women at Dean Park in another two-day encounter in 1951. The visitors again won comprehensively, by an innings and ten runs. New Zealand Women played a one-day fixture against Western Counties three years later. The home side were hanging on grimly at the end when they were nine in arrears in their second innings with two wickets remaining. The ground featured in the Women's World Cup of 1973. Australia Women proved far too strong for Young England Women, bowling them out for 53 and then knocking off the runs for the loss of three wickets.

THE COUNTY GROUND, SOUTHAMPTON

The County Ground first played host to women's cricket in July 1952, in a two-day match between England Women and The Rest. It was notable for an excellent century by 39-year-old Molly Hide, the most iconic figure in English women's cricket in the previous 20 years. She scored 141 not out in England's first innings of 222. The next highest score in the drawn match was 43. The next match on the ground in 1971 also featured an outstanding innings by a figure of similar stature. Rachel Flint (later Heyhoe-Flint) scored 83 in 93 minutes, the highest score of the match, for England Women against a Hampshire side. The one-day game was drawn. Heyhoe-Flint was a ground-breaker in that she was one of the first ten women admitted to MCC in 1999 as an honorary member at the instigation of Colin Ingleby-Mackenzie, honorary president of the club, and was elected to the full committee of MCC in 2004. She received an OBE in 2008 and became the only woman to be inducted to the ICC Hall of Fame in October 2010. A month later, she took her place as a Conservative Peer in the House of Lords. The first ODI at Southampton, and the last women's match to be played there, resulted in Australia Women overwhelming England Women by eight wickets in July 1998.

UNITED SERVICES GROUND, PORTSMOUTH

The Services staged their only women's match in 2005 when England played a warm-up match against England A, prior to their one-day series against India. England won by six wickets but batted on to give their batsmen further practice.

THE AGEAS BOWL

Hampshire's newest ground has so far staged two women's ODIs and two international Twenty20 matches. The former took place on successive days in August 2006. England beat India on both occasions, by three wickets and seven wickets respectively. In the first match, Sarah Taylor made 61 off 63 balls. Taylor showed her liking for the ground when she scored 73 off 66 balls against New Zealand in the first Twenty20 international in July 2010. However, the visitors held on to win the match by four wickets. New Zealand also provided the game's champagne moment when Sara McGlashan drove a massive six into the crowd over mid-off. England were more successful a year later when they defeated Australia Women by 16 runs. England again ran out winners when the two sides met on the ground last summer. The winning margin was five wickets, with Lydia Greenway scoring 80 not out.

THE AGEAS BOWL NURSERY GROUND

In May 2004, the top England players formed four sides, Super Strikers, Knight Riders, Braves and V Team, to contest a women's Twenty20 cricket contest with a view to preparing the country's elite players for international competition. The Knight Riders, captained by England skipper Charlotte Edwards, defeated the Super Strikers by four runs. The nursery ground has also staged County Championship matches for the Hampshire Senior Women's side and the county's under-age teams.

DISABILITY CRICKET

There are over 1,000 disabled participants playing at schools and clubs in Hampshire. There are county squads for people with a physical disability, people with a learning disability, people who have partial hearing and people with visual impairment.

NATIONAL DISABLED COUNTY CHAMPIONSHIP

After being runners-up in 2008, and reaching the semi-finals in the next two years, Hampshire won the National Disabled County Championship in 2012 by defeating Yorkshire by seven wickets in the final. Such was their superiority, they won with 25 overs to spare.

JEFF LEVICK MBE

Jeff Levick, who pioneered coaching of disability cricket in Hampshire, was awarded the MBE in the New Year's Honours List in 2012. The award was in recognition of his services to cricket. He has been involved as player and coach in grass-roots cricket for 50 years.

TWO DOUBLE CENTURIES IN A SEASON

Hampshire captain Jimmy Adams scored two double centuries: 219 not out against Worcestershire and 219 versus Northamptonshire, both at the Ageas Bowl in 1913. Only two other Hampshire batsmen have previously performed the feat. Philip Mead did so twice, in 1921 and 1922, and Gordon Greenidge in 1977.

ALAN RAYMENT – A UNIQUE ALL-ROUNDER

Alan Rayment was an attractive right-hand batsman who played in 198 matches from 1949 to 1958. His record was modest – 6333 runs (avge 20.36) including four centuries – mainly because he treated cricket as a game to be enjoyed. He would smile even when he had been dismissed for a duck. He was, though, a brilliant fielder in the covers, one of the best the county has possessed. Few cricketers can have pursued such a varied career outside of the game. During his county career he established his own dancing school in Southampton with his then wife. His CV then encompassed a summer on the coaching staff at Lord's where he turned down the job of head coach, estate agent, property developer, social worked, mature student and psychotherapist. He worked all over the world including Spain, Hawaii and the American mainland. After an absence of almost 50 years he returned to the Hampshire cricket scene by attending reunions and talking to Cricket Societies. In 2013, at the age of 85, he published the first volume of his memoirs, " Punchy ThroughThe Covers", a prodigious volume of 152,000 words covering only the first 21 years of his life. He has now started writing the second volume.

GORDON GREENIDGE RETAINED BY ONLY ONE VOTE

It seems surreal that Gordon Greenidge's contract was renewed by the casting vote of Hampshire's treasurer at the end of the 1969 season. The rest, as they say, is history. He made his Hampshire debut in the following year.

A FINAL MISCELLANY – CRICKET IN THE SOLENT

The most eccentric fixture played in Hampshire each year is the annual Brambles Cricket Match. It is contested by the Hamble and Island Yacht Clubs who race their craft to the middle of the Solent and begin to play as soon as the sea recedes enough to pitch stumps. The Brambles sandbank usually appears once a year, and allows play for about an hour. The yacht clubs even provide their own inn for the occasion, erecting a table and a few chairs for the doughty spectators. The participants in this surreal event are allegedly scarcely aware of the passing yachts and pleasure craft!